CHARGE UP YOUR PEOPLE!

27 Ways to Boost Performance

Giorgio Bicego, B.A.Sc., P.Eng.
Multiple Award Winning Author
www.chargeupyourpeoplebook.com
www.gbicego.com

Publisher
10-10-10 Publishing
Markham, ON   Canada
Printed in the United States of America
ISBN: 978-1-77277-128-2

Contents

DEDICATION

I dedicate this book to my sons Étienne, François, and Alexandre, and to my Liz whose love and support motivate me to live my life to the fullest every day, and to help them and as many people as possible along the way.

TESTIMONIALS

Giorgio has expanded company sales, improved cost structures, and increased business profits up to millions of dollars – he is professional, hard-working, and committed to delivering results.
Gianzo Mastrangelo, Vice President Sales – Brampton, ON

Giorgio identified improvement ideas within his first few days, further assessed our business needs, and then implemented initiatives, saving hundreds of thousands of dollars every year.
Robert Wallace, Plant Manager – Fergus, ON

Giorgio led our operations group, helping improve our employee safety, product/process quality, and productivity while improving OEEs (overall equipment effectiveness) by 15%+.
Stuart Faria, Plant Manager – Brampton, ON

Giorgio has extensive knowledge in the field of program management, ranging from quoting, driving formal business awards, commercial negotiations, supplier sourcing/purchasing, and liaising with both suppliers and customers while launching programs/processes on-time and on-budget.
Craig Clute, Program Manager – Newmarket, ON

Giorgio is a fantastic leader who is energetic, driven, and passionate in whatever he does; he is one of the best people I've ever worked for and always ensured we met our customer delivery requirements.
Gwen Crampton, Demand Planning – ERP Specialist – Toronto, ON

Giorgio is one of the most effective leaders I know; he is emotionally intelligent, wise, and a *people person* leader who guides and works well with all types of people while excelling in a wide variety of situations.
Aklilu Zere, Machine Division Manager – Etobicoke, ON

ACKNOWLEDGEMENTS

This book is a reflection in many ways of who I am and how I think in some areas of my life. Therefore, I first acknowledge my parents, Gianfranco and Vittoria, for immigrating to Canada and providing me an opportunity for a better life, and for loving and supporting me every step of the way. I also acknowledge my three sons—Étienne, François, and Alexandre—who mean the most to me and who I will always love much more than you know. I have always been, am, and will be, very proud of each and every one of you as you continue your own life journeys. I acknowledge my Liz who shares my life and whose love and support helps define me as the person I am and am becoming. I value my sister, Lisa, and her family, as well as all my cousins, aunts, and uncles, and long-time friends—Gianzo, Sebastijan, Frank, Tony, Anthony, Stuart, and others—who have always been with me throughout the good and the more challenging times.

I acknowledge and value my clients whom I've had the privilege of serving and helping with their businesses and lives. I thank my past employers who gave me an opportunity to support myself and family, and I acknowledge former work colleagues—Tom, Joseph, Richard, Ed, Hans, Glen, Carlo, Carolyn, Terry, Frank, Ana, Craig, Aklilu, Gwen, and Rob—who I now call friends.

I thank my coaches and mentors, Raymond Aaron, James Allen, Sir Richard Branson, Dr. Wayne Dyer, Napoleon Hill, Jim Rohn, Tony Robbins, and Oprah Winfrey. I also thank teachers from throughout my formal education—Mrs. Schweinberger, Mr. Vella, Mr. Hebor and Mr. Pascale—who taught me life lessons not included in their standard course curriculums.

I value and want to thank the people at The Raymond Aaron Group—Liz, Carla, Christina (for your help with the media kit and website), Rosa (for your extraordinary help as my book architect, answering my questions, and guiding me through this book writing journey), Helen and Mikee—and at 10-10-10 Publishing, who helped me put together and publish this book. A special thank you to Lisa who edited my books and makes my writing look great!

I apologize if I am forgetting anyone.

Finally, I acknowledge and thank you who have entrusted me with your time to read this book. I am humbled and grateful for the opportunity to share my ideas with you. Please contact me at www.chargeupyourbusinessbook.com and/or www.gbicego.com with your feedback, or to find out how I can help you and your business achieve your goals.

FOREWORD

I was very impressed when Giorgio told me he was writing his second book, *Charge Up Your People!: 27 Ways to Boost Performance*, at the same time as he was writing his first. Giorgio's decision to write and publish two books simultaneously is an example of his ability to meet challenges, and his dedication and commitment to helping you achieve your business goals.

Giorgio is honest, professional, and straightforward, and you will see this in what he teaches you within this book. Giorgio will explain to you how your people are key to your organization's success. He shares with you how to develop your business from a human resources point of view, and provides advice on how to support your employees from when they are first hired, to the end of their careers with your company.

After reading this book, I am certain that you will discover both new and experienced ideas and strategies that will help you to boost your people's performance. I urge you to contact Giorgio to help you achieve your business goals today!

Raymond Aaron
New York Times Bestselling Author

INTRODUCTION

Hello! Thank you for purchasing and reading this book! I wrote this book to offer my best advice and experiences in leading and working in successful businesses within several industries and throughout various parts of the world. As I began documenting my ideas and experiences in my original work, it became apparent that my manuscript was growing beyond my intentions in subjects and size. I also noticed my ideas supported two dominant themes I recommend and have always believed are necessary to lead any successful business: the science of running an organization (the *mechanics* of finance, operations, and continuous improvements), and the art of leadership and working with people (how to maximize your peoples' performances).

After considering advice from trusted friends and advisers, I decided to separate my original work into two books, each uniquely dedicated to focusing on the science of business and the art of leadership. I believe each of these two themes are so important, they deserve their own distinct book. The title of my other book is *Charge Up Your Business!: 27 Ways to Boost Profits* (www.chargeupyourbusiness book.com). You may consider the science of business as the foundation for your company operations and the art of leadership and working with people as the fuel that will propel your organization to achieve its goals.

This book is written for you who wants to learn and improve your leadership and people skills; I present many ideas and insights to enhance your talents and avoid potential catastrophes. Along the way, I have included my own personal business leadership and people experiences, highlighting various concepts. These ideas may be considered for your business regardless if you currently or plan to lead yourself, a small group, or large international groups of people striving to provide a product and/or service to your targeted market place(s).

Please send me your testimonials about this book and the ideas and concepts contained within. I always welcome your feedback of how these ideas and concepts have helped you and/or your business.

In the end, I cannot possibly anticipate and provide solutions in this book for every potential challenge faced by you and your business. I invite you to contact us at www.chargeupyourpeoplebook.com and/or www.gbicego.com if you would like more information and advice for your challenge(s), and how we can help you and your business achieve your goals and objectives.

CHAPTER 1

YOUR BUSINESS

What is Your Business?

The Merriam-Webster online dictionary defines business as "a usually commercial or mercantile activity engaged in as a means of livelihood." When I ask people to define their business, I typically receive responses ranging from what the product(s) and/or service(s) is/are produced by the business to what different people do in the business as part of their job(s). Sometimes I receive answers in the form of business objectives such as "we are here to make money," solving a social challenge, or involving where their business takes place, in a facility or on a website.

In my opinion, your business is the sum total of your own personal and other peoples' efforts to provide a unique value to meet a specific market demand in exchange for something of value to your business. A unique value to your market place can be anything—any service, product, or solution that solves a problem for your customers. Value in return for your business can be tangible such as money (revenue/sales), or intangible such as an exchange of services or a referral.

Considering my above definition, I propose a critical distinction between your business and anyone else's is you and your employees. Almost anyone can set up a website to compete with your website. Other people can also setup a business to compete with yours although you may have less competitors with increasing capital investment requirements. Even large multinational companies have competitors who may utilize similar marketing, customer service, manufacturing, and distribution techniques. Your, and your competitors', businesses may also provide some common features in your products and/or services because all humans share some common needs and characteristics. But one of the few ways businesses can differentiate themselves from each other is through their people, their employees, core values, goals, and objectives. I suggest to you that most differentiating factors for your business—what makes it unique—is directly linked to the unique group of people who lead, and work in and with your business.

The Four Stages of Your Business

Life can be thought of as a series of phases or stages. Think of the seasons: spring, summer, fall, and winter. Think of a person's life: birth, childhood, adolescence, adulthood, and death. Your business also experiences stages: start-up, growth, stabilization, and its end. Each business stage requires a different set of priorities, activities, strategies, resources, and leadership styles—let me explain below.

Your business start-up phase can be a very exciting and simultaneously daunting time. Your personal and business lives may seem to merge as you perhaps may be working long hours, six to seven days a week, working out of a garage, basement, or your bedroom, just as some (now) famous business leaders began their companies. You may have one or a few customers, very little capital, and very few (if any) employees during this time. I recommend it is very critical during your start-up stage (as in all stages but much more critical here) that you do not over extend yourself and your business in terms of commitments regarding your time, energy, and, most importantly, cash flow and expenses. It may be easier to focus on your one or a few customers at this point, but I recommend that you ensure they do not monopolise all your time and resources more than is required.

You've survived your business start-up phase—congratulations! Now it's time to grow your business, expand your customer base, perhaps get some help, and/or more resources. This is an exciting time for you and your business but also filled with potential pitfalls such as miscalculating how many new sales and customers you and your business can potentially absorb in the foreseeable future and/or how much support you may need to support those new sales and customers. I suggest it's relatively easy to say "yes" to that big new contract, but then your business needs to deliver upon its commitments; that's when it can become challenging unless your business is properly setup and prepared to absorb those new sales. I recommend it is critical during your business growth stage to surround yourself with a few but important people to help you and your business deliver your product and/or service with the expected quality, cost, and on time. I also recommend you consider hiring people during your growth stage who share some of your entrepreneurial characteristics and strengths such as high energy, dedication, and a willingness to take on a variety of tasks in a multi-priority environment.

Now that you've survived both your start-up and growth stages, I suggest it's time to allow your company to enter its business stabilization phase. This stage may be characterized by a slower growth rate and a more *manageable* pace (if your business can afford that). Hopefully you still have your health, family, customers, and most of your employees at this point. Your business stabilization stage is a time to allow your business and employees to catch their breath, but it can also be filled with potential challenges. I caution you that this can be a time where some businesses may trace their initial steps leading to eventual bankruptcy because they and their employees were tempted to "sit back and get fat." Perhaps you may feel you can afford that odd *luxury* time away from your marketplace or incur expenses that may or may not benefit yourself, business, or employees. I recommend you always remain careful with your time and money, especially during your stabilization stage when it may seem you may finally have some "extra" to spare. I also advise you determine and maintain the appropriate balance between your business growth and stabilization activities to support your company's long term growth.

Your business stabilization stage is a time when you can increase your focus to standardize and maximize efficiencies in every aspect of your business. Perhaps you may need to hire additional people but different from yourself, i.e. perhaps not as entrepreneurial as those employees you hired and retained during and since your business growth stage. I suggest your *stabilization stage* people will maintain and improve your business processes and are just as important to your business as your growth stage people. At the same time, I recommend you need to keep your *growth stage* employees engaged and interested in their work or risk losing them. Every one of your employees has their role, and one type of employee is no more important than another. Your business needs both *stabilization* and *growth* employees since one may not complete tasks as effectively as the other, but only together may propel your business over the long term. Once you've achieved your business stabilization goals, I suggest it's time to re-emphasize your business growth activities. Continuous, repeated, and successful transitions between successive growth and stabilization phases will ensure your business's long term success.

As with many aspects in life, there is usually an end for every beginning. The end of your business (when you own it) may occur when you decide to sell it to another party, caused by your own death (if you are a sole proprietor) or insolvency. The "end" of an era in an existing business may be caused by a senior leadership change and/or a significant market event(s) and may be an opportunity for a new start or direction for the business. Whatever the cause(s) leading to your business end stage, I recommend you reflect upon your business lessons learned and progress to your next opportunity(ies).

During your business end stage, I advise it is critical that you wind down your activities in an orderly fashion as much as possible. I also advise you inform your employees, customers, and suppliers (in that order) as soon as possible about your business end plans. I recommend it is important during your business end phase (and at all times) to thank your employees, customers, and suppliers for their loyalty and to treat them with respect and fairness. It is also important during this time to help your employees as much as possible with their next phases of work and personal lives.

Each one of your four business stages requires different leadership and management styles and priorities from yourself and your leadership team. And each business phase requires its own different capital requirements and types of people to support the major area(s) of focus during each stage. I recommend that you, as the business leader, need to constantly balance both your business short-term and long-term objectives to ensure your business's long term success. One very important business leadership skill is to recognize your current business stage and act accordingly, while simultaneously planning for your next business stage—this is an example of true business leadership and the topic of the next chapter.

For More Information and Advice

Please contact us at www.chargeupyourpeoplebook.com and/or www.gbicego.com if you would like more information and advice for your business, your business stages and/or any other challenges—we are here to help.

CHAPTER 2

LEADERSHIP

An Introduction to Leadership

What is leadership, and what characteristics define a true leader? There seem to be a variety of leadership styles and leaders in every aspect of life. Perhaps you are a leader in business, at your workplace, in politics, or in the military, but there also are leadership positions in other aspects of life such as at home, within a group of relatives or friends, a classroom, or on a sports team. Some people strive to be leaders while others reluctantly find themselves in a position of leadership, whereas many people are content to be followers. I suggest leadership is the art of guiding and supporting other people while mastering five skills: vision or strategy, goal setting, execution or tactics, delegation, and follow-up.

I recall a conversation about leadership that made an impression on me and forms part of my own leadership style. I was out on the production floor one afternoon having a conversation with our general manager while we were observing how our employees were working with a new process. He told me one of his key responsibilities was to ensure the company supported its employees both directly and indirectly in all aspects of their lives. For example, he felt personally responsible to ensure employees had opportunities to make their rent and mortgage payments, car payments, and support their children. Although you may reflect on this or a similar philosophy before making any business decision(s) involving people, I recommend you always, as do I, decide on what is best for the business in the medium and long terms.

An important leadership requirement is courage to always do what is best for your business first, even if that decision may affect you personally and/or may not be popular with other people. And by your business, I mean your entire group of employees, customers, and suppliers in that order of priority. I recommend your every decision as a business leader must be made to ensure your company's ongoing survival and improvement. Some of your business decisions may seem "easy" if there are financial and/or other resources to support them, such as improving employee benefits, adding new equipment and/or adding people after, or in anticipation of, new orders. Sometimes you, as a business leader, may need to make tougher decisions such as having to lay off employees due to uncontrollable market conditions, or terminate a person's employment—or perhaps it may benefit your business (and you personally) that you fire yourself!

Do you have what it takes to be an effective leader? Can you communicate a vision, resolve problems, and inspire and motivate other people while focusing on results? Can you plan, focus, think about the long term while considering the short term, and can you effectively delegate to and follow-up with people? Are you honest, confident, positive, transparent, and open-minded? Do you have integrity, and are you adaptable, empathetic, driven, accountable, and able to assess sometimes complicated issues and then make a decision(s)? Be honest with yourself. If you do, great! If you do not possess some or all of these leadership qualities and skills at the moment, that's okay too. Perhaps you may need to learn, practice, and incorporate a few more leadership qualities and skills into your leadership style. Or perhaps you may not want to be a leader in a certain aspect of your life—that's fine too. With your desire, courage, and self-confidence to be a leader, I suggest you can develop and improve your leadership skills by practising them at every opportunity and in increasing amounts. In my opinion, there are at least five essential skills for effective leadership: vision or strategy, goal setting, execution or tactics, delegation, and follow-up. Let's discuss these skills in further detail.

Vision / Strategy

Creating a vision for your business is critical. Without a vision, you may have no idea about your business's current state and future direction. You may have heard some sayings such as "a boat without a destination always remains in port" or "a ship without a rudder will eventually crash onto the rocks"—these are all true in my opinion.

Before creating a vision for yourself and your business, I recommend it is important that you first establish both your personal and your business values—many of which may be similar if not identical. Typically, your core business values may reflect your own personal values. This is an extraordinary benefit of being a business leader, that you can create a business whose core values reflect your own. For example, your business core values may include honesty, integrity, accountability, customer focus, helping others, respect, and fairness. To determine your personal and/or business values, ask yourself questions such as, "What characteristics are important to me? What characteristics do I aspire to? How would I like to live my personal and/or business life?" I recommend asking a spouse, family member, friend, advisor, or coach if you are having trouble determining your own personal and/or business values— tell them to be brutally honest! If you don't like their answers, you may need to reflect who you really are at the moment and may need to make some changes. After confirming your business values, you have now created the foundation upon which you can build your business vision.

Creating a business vision is critical leadership work that may require some time and reflection. I suggest your overall business vision will eventually come to life as a result of your thinking, reflection, and research, and will set the foundation for all future work in your business. I recommend you begin this process by thinking about what market need(s) your business may fulfill and your priorities during every stage of your business development. You may realize there could be an endless stream of possible scenarios and answers to these questions. You may also find it helpful to write down your thoughts to begin clarifying your thinking and eventually define a developing pattern(s) or theme(s). You may also find it helpful to ask trusted friends, advisors, potential business partners, or currently recognized leaders in your business marketplace. Your resultant business vision can then be summarized and documented, with a mission statement posted in your office and throughout your company facility(ies).

Your business vision does not need to be cast in stone, and you may need to consider changing or improving it to reflect changes within your business and market place(s). On the other hand, I recommend you seriously consider any change(s) to your business values since they are the foundations of your business vision and business itself. Especially when it may seem tempting to do so, it requires unshakeable courage to stick to your core business values in the face of challenges that may even threaten the very existence of your business itself. I suggest your business may survive and grow through just about any adversity(ies), depending on the strength of your business core values and your, as well as your employees', personal commitments to them. I recommend it is critical as a business leader that you review both your core business values and business vision on a regular basis to ensure your business activities remain focused to supporting both of them.

Goal Setting

After deciding upon your core values and creating a vision, I recommend your next step is to create goals and action plans to support your business and its priorities. Your business goals will guide you and your team in your everyday activities to achieve your business vision and priorities, and will also give you an opportunity to measure your progress.

You may be wondering how to effectively establish goals for your entire business team, and how you can attain everyone's *buy-in* or commitment to achieve them. One common method is where you personally devise goals for each of your business departments and then share them with your senior leaders. You may need to convince your senior leadership about achieving these goals or eventually resort to "telling" them these goals must be achieved. Your senior leadership then repeats this process with their employees. I suggest this method may have limited success in the short term and requires a great deal of follow-up activities on your part. There is an alternative process or philosophy that may seem similar in some ways to this methodology but fundamentally different in other aspects, that is proven to improve adherence to your business vision and priorities over the long term.

An alternate policy deployment process shares your overall business vision and priorities with all the levels of your organization, aids to obtain all your employees' commitments, and assists in the development of goals throughout your entire organization to achieve your business vision. Your policy deployment process starts with you, as the business leader, determining your business vision and priorities for the upcoming year. Your second step consists of a series of conversations between yourself, as the business leader, and your senior leadership team to establish their area of responsibility goals that align with and achieve your business vision and priorities. These series of conversations and exercises are referred to as the *catch ball* process. I want to point out that in this process, unlike the previous one, it is your senior leadership who proposes their goals to align themselves with your business priorities or vision for the upcoming year—not you telling them what their goals are/will be. This is also a time where both parties may need to negotiate as you work with your senior leadership's suggestions until you reach a consensus where their goals are established and aligned with your business vision/priorities. The third step occurs when your senior leadership team duplicates this *catch ball* process with their direct-report employees—let's say your department managers. The result of this third step is the establishment of department goals that are aligned with your senior leadership's goals, which are in turn aligned with your own business vision and priorities. The fourth, and perhaps last step, occurs when your department managers repeat this process with their individual employees, once again establishing individual employee goals that eventually align themselves with your overall business priorities and vision. I suggest implementing this policy deployment method will enhance the chances that your business vision and priorities will remain consistent throughout your entire organization although each employee's individual goals and methods may differ to achieve your overall business vision and priorities.

A popular goal setting method is summarized by the acronym SMART; I suggest developing goals that follow the SMART requirements increases your chances of achieving them. "S" stands for *specific*—your intended result needs to be as specific as possible. The more specific your goal statement is, the more likely you will achieve the goal. "M" stands for *measurable*—your goal must be stated in a way where its result can be verified by others. For example, a specific target number or date is more effective than stating you will improve a measurable. "A" stands for *achievable*—your goal must realistic. For example, if you've just started your bakery business with a single small shop, a business goal to generate twenty-five million dollars in annual revenue may be considered too steep or unrealistic at the moment, whereas this same goal for a large international organization may seem to be too easy to achieve. I recommend you set goals that are achievable and require you to stretch yourself and your resources to achieve them—avoid unreasonably easy and "pie in the sky" goals. "R" stands for *relevant*—your goal should be related or have meaning for your business vision. For example, a business goal for your bakery to start operations open to the public by a certain date is relevant, whereas volunteering to coach a local sports team after work may not be a relevant business goal. "T" stands for *time*—by what specific date (and/or sometimes the time of that date) your goal will be achieved. I suggest your goal suddenly becomes *real* every time you complete this goal setting step of setting a deadline; I think it's because you've now committed to a specific date in the future that you know you cannot change or prevent from happening. You can modify any of the other "S", "M", "A", or "R" aspect(s) of SMART goal setting, but neither you nor anyone can stop time "T" from happening.

Execution / Tactics

One of the best ways I recommend, and practice myself, to maximize the chances of achieving business goals is to involve others in designing and then implementing those goals. This practice is highlighted in the policy deployment methodology described in the previous section. Ask yourself how dedicated you will be to achieving a goal that you were not a part of designing. Or, even worse, a goal that you are not even involved in implementing? Get the picture? I assume you may have heard of *employee involvement* or *employee empowerment*, and how many business leaders "preach" about these concepts but rarely or never effectively practice them. I suggest many business leaders may not yet have the courage and/or trust to allow their employees to actually be empowered in their day-to-day job activities—how sad. I suggest these same employees, who may not yet be "trusted" to be empowered at work, are the same people who may lead families, other people and organizations, and achieve extraordinary goals outside of work. I have always believed and recommend you involve as many people as appropriate when designing business goals and implementing action plans to achieve them.

I suggest another critical successful goal attainment strategy is to break up a large goal into a series of smaller goals or steps to achieve the larger goal's objective. A large goal may seem intimidating and/or nearly impossible to achieve within current constraints of time, efforts, and other resources. Once you break up your overall larger goal plan into smaller steps or sub-goals, each with its own sub-target date(s) within your overall major goal target date, you and your team can then focus on achieving those simpler sub-goals. Consistent and on-time attainment of all your project sub-goals will eventually result in achieving your overall project goal(s).

Delegate, Delegate, Delegate

How many people do you need to fly an airplane? Many people may answer, "One," focusing on the pilot. It is true that the pilot flies the plane, especially if they are flying a small one, but larger commercial jets have more than one person in their cockpit. In addition to a pilot and co-pilot, there are other people required to allow an airplane to fly, such as the airplane mechanic(s), ground crew, fuelling person(s), air traffic controllers, and other airport personnel. Without all these other people in addition to the pilot and co-pilot, no commercial airplane would ever leave the ground.

The above example demonstrates that no great achievement can be attained, let alone sustained, without the help of others. Consider remarkable achievements such as landing on the moon or the development of the Internet—they were achieved through team work and delegation. Even to complete a simple task as going to work, you still need an auto mechanic and fuel station personnel, or a public transportation driver and their mechanics to help take you there. So why do some people from time to time think, "If you want the job done right, you have to do it yourself?" I suggest many business leaders may not effectively delegate for several reasons; they may not trust others to complete the task(s). There are, of course, certain legal and financial tasks that only you as the business leader should complete. But if you feel you cannot delegate a certain task to someone, I suggest you may have a trust issue and/or the other person may not be qualified to complete the task. Either way, I recommend it is in your and other person's best interests that you resolve this issue as soon as possible. I suggest another reason for not delegating tasks to others may be "it takes too much time to train and delegate to others"—typically this excuse is used by those who seem to have very little time and are always rushing through their days. I suggest this reasoning counteracts a leader's effectiveness because it is those very people who rush throughout their days that may need to delegate tasks so they can focus on more value-added activities.

I propose delegation benefits both parties—let's call them the *delegator* (the one who delegates the task) and the *delegatee* (the person to whom the task is delegated). Delegation is a win-win: the delegator frees up more of their time to focus on other more valued added tasks and increase their own productivity while the delegatee also increases their value added activities. The following personal experience demonstrates how I came to appreciate the value of delegation. At a time when I was currently responsible for a process engineering department, a consultant hired by our president asked me to consider fulfilling the plant manager role. After accepting his proposal, the consultant told me there was one obstacle to this plan: my engineering team currently could not function without me. In essence, I had not yet delegated enough of my tasks (that I insisted on completing personally) to my team to allow me to pursue this promotion. Within six weeks, I delegated all my process engineering tasks and accepted my new promotion.

Although you may not be able to delegate every task in a project or endeavour, I recommend you practice delegation as much as possible at every available opportunity to free up your time and focus on more value added and productive activities within your business. As an added benefit, practising the critical leadership skill of delegation also allows those people to whom you've delegated responsibilities, to increase their value to your business—everyone wins.

Follow-up, Follow-up, Follow-up

Another critical leadership requirement is following-up with your people to ensure the effective implementation of your business vision and priorities. Follow-up is perhaps the best leadership strategy to provide constant feedback on your business's direction and its rate of progress. Without your follow-up as the business leader, chaos may slowly begin to creep into and derail your business efforts. Despite its importance, many business leaders typically do not spend enough time to effectively follow-up on their major business initiatives. I suggest effective follow-up is usually the last missing link that many business leaders simply ignore and/or leave to others to complete follow-up on their behalf. I don't know why; perhaps the idea of follow-up may not be as interesting or appealing as other elements of business leadership, or perhaps some business leaders may be too bothered by follow-up, preferring to "delegate and forget." Then it may turn out those same business "leaders" are surprised and frustrated that something went very wrong, and their business may be in serious trouble.

One key element for effective follow-up is to listen to what your people are telling you even if you don't want to hear it—this may be more challenging than you think. Another requirement for effective follow-up is you may need to verify some information for yourself. You may think of this concept as "I trust you, but I will verify," and may consider replying in such a manner if a concerned employee asks about your follow-up reason(s). I suggest you reassure people the purpose for your follow-up is not that you do not trust them, but that you follow-up to ensure solutions and activities are effectively implemented. I also recommend you consider regular *follow-up walks* or *visits*; perhaps you can also schedule these events into your calendar as a reminder. You may also, on occasion, consider to conduct surprise follow-up walks or visits without warning, depending on your corporate culture, business objectives, and perception of how well your organization is achieving your business priorities or lack thereof.

Sometimes a rare surprise follow-up visit may benefit your organization by refocusing people's attention on a particular priority(ies) while creating some "needed" animosity or to "shake things up". But I also caution that repeated, unannounced surprise visits may or will usually "backfire" by creating a negative indifference amongst those people whom you wish to influence in the first place. In that case, I recommend you cease all surprise follow-up visits and approach those people in a more effective manner(s).

Leading by Example

An additional crucial requirement for effective leadership is the practice of leading by example, i.e. do what I do. Put simply, leading by example provides you, as a business leader, tremendous credibility and respect from your employees. Leading by example also demonstrates your respect for your employees. Without credibility and respect for and from your employees, I suggest you will quickly become an ineffective "lame duck" leader as a result of following the alternative, ineffective, and unfortunately more common practice of "do what I say."

Too many business "leaders" have lectured and sometimes disciplined employees for certain actions and then personally performed, or worse, allowed others to carry out those same actions. A business "leader" will send conflicting messages to their company and will instantly and permanently lose credibility and respect from their employees if they ever practice the "do what I say, not what I do" philosophy. Business "leaders" will be accused of favouritism and/or being a hypocrite if they allow some people to act in a certain way(s) and try to hold others accountable for the same or similar action(s). It's a lose-lose situation: employees lose credibility and respect for their "leader" who in turn quickly and permanently loses their leadership effectiveness.

It may require only one single incident of "do what I say, not what I do" to lose your credibility and respect for and from your employees, and you as a business leader may never recover from that incident. It's a very high bar set for business leaders that they must always practice leading by example. Your effectiveness as a business leader may improve with time if some or most of your employees forget or ignore your last "do what I say, not what I do" incident. But I suggest any subsequent "do what I say, not what I do" incident will further reduce, and quickly and perhaps permanently destroy any chance(s) of recovering your effectiveness as a business leader. You may consider peoples' opinions of your actions as a business leader to be harsh and unfair at times, and that may be true. I suggest you may not be cut out for or have what it takes to be an effective business leader if you are considering the leading by example "bar" may be set too high.

So what can you do if you've been caught committing, or what others seem to think you've committed, a "do what I say, not what I do" action? I suggest business leaders will further reduce their credibility and respect for and from their employees whenever they attempt to ignore, hide, or *sweep under the carpet*, an action contradictory to an established policy or practice. Even worse, I suggest such actions may also breed contempt from their employees—not a good situation.

Whenever you've "slipped up" and genuinely committed a mistake, I recommend you consider admitting you made a mistake and move on. I suggest most of your employees will be happy to continue working for you and continue respecting your leadership authority as long as your admission is sincere and that any mistake(s) occur on a rare basis. There may be at times a valid reason(s) when you may need to defend your action(s), citing a special situation or an exception to the rule which may be valid under reasonable circumstances. In this case, I recommend you offer a clarification(s) to dispel any confusion and complete any modification(s) to an existing policy and/or practice that will be valid going forward. These actions are the only way in my opinion to regain your leadership credibility and respect for and from your employees.

Leadership Responsibility & Authority

I suggest effective leadership can never exist if a person is in a position of full responsibility with little or no authority to execute changes within their area(s) of responsibility(ies). Put simply, I propose that full leadership responsibility without full leadership authority does not work. Leadership responsibility without authority is like mixing water and oil, pushing a square peg through a round hole, or driving a car or riding a bicycle with square wheels—extremely difficult to do, if not impossible, and just not worth your efforts.

Authority or power, or at least the perception of authority or power, over other people can be addictive as witnessed in history or by examples in our current society and in our own personal lives. The perception of authority or power over people may supply some people's ego who in my opinion may have a low self-esteem and/or low opinion of others. Some business leaders may freely delegate responsibilities to others but, for some reason, delegating (or what some think of as giving up) authority poses a challenge. I propose leaders who refuse to delegate responsibility with authority may have decided their personal ego is more important—very sad for them and their people. I suggest your effectiveness as a business leader is limited by your authority to act accordingly in any area of responsibility.

I suggest your business leadership authority may be more widely accepted at the beginning of your time of leadership, but then must be earned through your decisions and actions to reinforce your leadership credibility and thus authority. Similar to the practice of leading by example, I recommend every decision and action affects your leadership authority, credibility, and respect for and from your employees. This concept is another example of the "high bar" expectation set for leaders. I suggest it may only require one or a few bad decision(s) and/or action(s) to begin undermining your leadership authority and credibility despite many past good decisions and actions.

I also recommend you establish different authority levels within your business to ensure its efficient operations, or chaos may ensue in very short order. This can be done by creating a *chain of command* and enforcing it in almost every situation unless someone's personal safety or your business existence may be at stake. I suggest one of the worst things you can do as a business leader is intentionally or unintentionally, directly or indirectly, undermine your own and/or someone else's authority.

You may have seen or personally experienced when full leadership responsibility has been assigned and achieved with full leadership authority, but then some or all authority was controlled or taken away at the first sign of anything going wrong or for no apparent reason(s) at all. A retraction of authority may be subtle or very apparent to the leader reducing someone's authority, their sub-leader whose authority is being reduced, and everyone else. The road to authority reduction may start with an event as subtle as just listening or entertaining the opinion of a sub-leader's employee and committing to do something. Before doing so, I advise you always ask that employee if they've discussed the issue(s) with their supervisor. If they haven't, I suggest you do nothing and advise that employee to approach their direct supervisor before returning back to you in case their supervisor has not addressed their concern(s) appropriately.

Micromanaging can be a subtle strategy to limit a person's authority. In some cases, what may appear as micromanaging may be necessary at times, especially if your organization is experiencing a scarcity of resources or any other kind of serious crisis. And in some circumstances, some people prefer to be micromanaged. But I suggest most micromanaging cases may be attempts to limit someone else's authority and activities, and an indication of poor leadership, delegation, and follow-up (too much follow-up) skills on the part of the person who is trying to micromanage someone else. I recommend, unless your business is in a temporary and severe crisis, that you avoid micromanaging anyone in their activities.

A consequence of micromanaging and exercising your authority over your sub-leaders and their employees is that you will also inherit their responsibilities and their headaches! Effective leadership requires both full responsibility and authority. I suggest that a modification to the saying "if you want something done, do it yourself" should be "if you want something done right, do it yourself, but then be prepared to assume responsibilities and headaches in addition to those you already have!" I also suggest that assuming others' authority and responsibilities may eventually affect your own effectiveness as a business leader.

Whenever you, as the business leader, notice or become aware of an issue within a sub-leader's area of responsibility, I recommend you address this issue with your sub-leader in a private one to one conversation as soon as possible. You may conclude, after speaking with your sub-leader, that you misinterpreted the perceived situation, thus avoiding a potentially critical mistake of *taking over*. I suggest another reason to avoid taking over your sub-leader's area of responsibility, while still retaining them in your organization, is to avoid rendering your sub-leader as an ineffective "lame duck" who you now need to pay while they are no longer performing their job responsibilities. Instead of satisfying your own ego, I suggest you consider doing the *right* thing by speaking with your sub-leader and offering advice and training, if feasible, to help them improve their performance and results. If those strategies do not seem to work, I recommend it may be time to remove your sub-leader from your business with respect and fairness.

Leadership vs. Management

The concepts of *leadership* and *management* may be interchanged and used in the same context at times since both leaders and managers need to support and work with other people to achieve their business objectives. I propose every leader is a manager, but not every manager can be a leader. So what's the difference between *leadership* and *management*? I suggest leaders primarily focus on what and why, and then perhaps on when, who, and how, whereas managers primarily focus on when, who, and how, and then perhaps on what and why when dealing with a challenge, initiative, or situation. To put it another way, a leader sets policies or initiatives, and a manager ensures the implementation of those policies or initiatives. I also suggest a person needs to learn and practice supervisor or manager skills before they can act as an effective leader.

I recommend your business needs both leaders and managers to ensure its long term success, while at the same time one is not better or preferred over the other. Some people may place more importance on leaders, but I suggest every great leader acknowledges that their effectiveness is enhanced by the support of their managers and team(s) who support their priorities. I also recommend that not everyone should and can be a leader in your business—nothing will effectively get done. Let me explain using a personal experience. I attended a leadership workshop where all us typical "leaders" were placed in a group and asked to devise a plan to meet a challenge. Our result: we "leaders" spent most of our time arguing and trying to direct each other, achieved nothing, and finished last of the four teams who participated in the exercise. Some business leaders may send their company into chaos if they tried to assume some manager tasks, while some managers may be down-right fearful and/or negligent if they tried to lead a business. In my opinion, your business requires a balance of both leaders and managers. I propose that an essential requirement for senior, effective business leadership is to recognize who is a potential leader and who may be a potential manager in your company, and allow your employees grow into the role(s) they wish to play in your organization.

Your True Leadership Test

Some business leaders may think they have passed their true leadership test when everyone does what is told or expected of them. I suggest this thinking is reminiscent of a *top down* leadership style that in my opinion may not be as effective at times as a *servant leadership* style to achieve business goals. I recommend you consider that collaborative efforts from everyone in your business supported by your servant-type leadership style may be an effective strategy to ensure your business's long term and sustainable growth. I also advise you to consider that your true test of effective leadership is what happens in your company when you are actually NOT physically present and involved in your business. Can your business sustain and can your people overcome any problems (that typically you may handle) even if you're not there or involved? I suggest your job as a business leader is done if you can honestly answer "yes" to this question. I also recommend you may still have some leadership work to do if your answer is anything but a definite "yes." Let me demonstrate my point with a personal experience.

Early in my career, I was accepted to attend a business leadership and operations program at a prominent university. This was no retreat: every minute of our sixteen hour days were filled with scheduled exercises, classes, and study group sessions, seven days a week, lasting almost four weeks. It was challenging for all participants to be away from their business and work responsibilities for such a long period of time. During these weeks, just about every participant was contacted almost on a daily basis by their business associates— everyone except me. I didn't receive one phone call at their office (cell phones were not readily available at that time), not one message on my pager, or any written message (posted on a large easel) to call anyone at my business. I finally called my supervisor, our business vice president, two days before the program end, asking how the business was functioning in my absence. He flippantly replied, pretending not to recognize me—yikes! Then our vice president told me he almost contacted me on two occasions but was so impressed how my supervisors resolved issues on their own (as I trained them to do so) that no phone calls were deemed necessary. In fact, he jestingly stated the business seemed to run better without me! In that same light-hearted mood, I replied that if the business was running so well without me, he could certainly approve my registration for another similar thirteen week training program set to commence before month's end! After we shared some laughter, the vice president asked me to return after my training to begin working on new major business initiatives.

As demonstrated by my personal experience above, I suggest you will have passed your true leadership test when your business and employees can effective run your company without your presence and involvement. Once you've effectively removed yourself from your business day-to-day operations, I recommend that you may focus on more strategic business and/or career challenges.

Some Final Thoughts on Leadership

As I have already mentioned, I recommend you as a business leader must hold yourself and other leaders to a *higher* level of expectations associated with leadership. I am not suggesting that you should consider yourself "better" than anyone else. What I mean by *higher* level of leadership expectations is you cannot afford to be petty, play political games, and focus on short-term issues that may not affect your business's long term survival and growth.

I also recommend that this higher level of leadership expectations means you should always think, say, and do what is right for your business and your employees, even if it is to your own personal detriment. These higher expectation levels only increase as your business leadership stature rises within your organization. My advice is to remove yourself from your leadership position for the benefit of the business if you cannot accept and live by these higher expectations. Similarly, if you as a leader notice a sub-leader cannot and/or is not willing accept higher leadership expectations, my advice is to speak with and coach/train them to correct their behaviours. If those strategies don't seem to correct the situation, I recommend you similarly remove that sub-leader since they may degrade and/or destroy your company employee morale.

As a business leader, I recommend you need to be aware that everyone else (your employees, customers, and suppliers) are constantly watching you, noting your every decision and action, big or small, every statement and word that you speak and how you do so, your daily habits, your moods, what issues excite you, and what issues anger you. This surveillance and sometimes criticism (even if it doesn't seem fair and/or seems personal at times) never seems to end when you are a leader. Depending on your leadership level and effectiveness, your entire business operations may "ride" or function according to your personal mood and actions, even if you are not personally present or involved at the time.

I also recommend that you, as the business leader, consider taking more time off than others in your company to maintain a balanced state of mind and ensure you make effective business decisions. After your business has been established, you may not be able to afford to "put your nose to the grindstone" as others may do. Your business leadership role typically requires more mental than physical efforts, sometimes beyond commonly accepted regular working hours. I also suggest that being in good physical shape, getting a good sleep, taking a walk during the day, taking off a morning or an afternoon away from the office, or a long weekend, will ensure you have the stamina, mental strength, and perspectives required to make good business decisions. I suggest you will return to your business more refreshed, relaxed, and able to tackle ongoing issues with more focus and clarity of thought after any significant time away. Who knows, maybe your employees may also enjoy their time at work while you are away!

One final thought on leadership: it may seem at times that anyone can lead your business in *good times* when things are going well, like steering a ship in good weather—it may seem effortless and easy from an outsider's point of view to occupy the leadership seat or sit in the captain's chair. This perception may seem like a logical conclusion by an outsider since they may typically be unaware of and/or forget about your hard work, time, and efforts invested into a business to ensure it reached the point where it runs smoothly. I suggest your true business leadership skills will be revealed and recognized whenever your business is in a crisis or the ship hits "rough seas." As in business and life, actions speak louder than words. During times of crisis, I recommend your key business leader responsibilities are to remain calm and assuring, take care of your employees, customers, and suppliers while remaining focused on developing and implementing a solutions(s) as soon as possible. I also recommend that you identify lesson(s) learned from a crisis and incorporate them into your business practices to prevent any potential calamities.

For More Information and Advice

Please contact us at www.chargeupyourpeoplebook.com and/or www.gbicego.com if you would like more information and advice for your leadership challenges such as vision/strategy, goal setting, execution/tactics, delegation, follow-up, leading by example, leadership authority and responsibility, leadership vs. management, your true leadership test and/or any other challenges—we are here to help.

CHAPTER 3

YOUR PEOPLE

Who is the Most Important Person in Your Company?

Who is the most important person in your organization to achieve its goals? This was a question posed to me and our class of approximately seventy-five business executives selected from over fifteen hundred applicants from around the world, at a business leadership and operations program held at a prestigious university business school. As the youngest participant in this training, I immediately stood up and declared my response, "The person who is actually doing the work on the line or delivering the service—thank you very much!" and sat down. I could not have predicted that my response, the first one, started a debate that at times seemed would never end. I spent the next ninety or so minutes debating with just about every other classmate who disagreed with me, especially a senior executive who was a senior vice president of a very large and well known multi-international company. Most of my classmates stated the CEO was the most important person in a business because they set company directions and priorities. Others replied customers were the most important people in any business because they were the source of revenue, or management because they ensured the implementation of directions and priorities. In fact, near the end of the debate, the senior professor in attendance poured me a glass of water since I was beginning to lose my voice. That same professor then thanked us for our participation and expressing our views, and referred to a very thick and extensive study recently completed over a two-year period by some of the top business consultants, or *gurus*, at the time, who are still recognized today as leaders in the field of business strategies and management. The professor then read the conclusion of this study and answered this question: the most important person in a business is that individual(s) who actually completes the value added work and/or delivers the service to the end customer(s). Everyone applauded while the senior professor again walked toward my seat extending his hand to congratulate me for my answer.

Unless your business is a "one-person show," I advise you will need other peoples' help to achieve your business goals. If not, I suggest your business growth may be limited by your own personal time, efforts, and resources—for some people, that may be exactly how they want to run their business. I have met many business leaders who are in business for themselves and have no employees. I also know business leaders who hired new, or inherited current, employees and eventually terminated them permanently or rehired them as contractors. Whatever your preference(s), I propose your business objectives will determine if and how many employees you will need to hire in your company. Regardless if you have employees or not, I also suggest you will eventually need at least some people involved in your business, either as customers and/or suppliers.

This chapter may be the most important one in the entire book, not only if you currently have, or plan to have, employees, but also because you must eventually interact with other people to conduct your business. I recommend you consider that people—your employees, your associates, your partners, your teammates, whatever you call them—are your most important business resource. Some business leaders say their people "are their most important asset" but then act in ways that contradict this philosophy. Be honest with yourself—really honest. Do you treat your people as well as you can, or do you think of them as *subservient staff*? Do you create and communicate a business vision for or with your employees' support, or do you at times consider them as a *necessary evil*? Do you sincerely listen to your employees' ideas, complaints at times, or just regard them as a cost of *doing business*? Let's face it; without other people, your business will fail! Even if you're a single-person entrepreneur, you still need other people—at least customers and perhaps suppliers—to thrive in business. Forget about business for a moment. I suggest success in life (and business) is determined by your belief and acting upon a simple universal truth: true and long lasting happiness is found in the service of others.

Employee Morale

I suggest that without good personal morale, you're toast—it's tough to do anything well. Similarly, I suggest without good employee morale, you're business is toast—your employees will not perform at their maximum potentials. As critical as employee morale is to any business success, it may not be easy for some people to accurately measure it. I suggest employee morale can be measured as a sense of what's going on in your company and how your employees are feeling overall about you, the business, or about each other. I advise that you, as a business leader, should always be aware of its current state. In fact, I recommend you consider that your employee morale is one of the most important, and perhaps the most important, business measurable of all. More important than profits? More important than sales? Hear me out for a moment.

With good employee morale, I suggest your people may come to work, openly and sincerely volunteer their ideas and opinions, and find ways to solve problems. With good employee morale, I propose your people may work more safely and ensure the quality and delivery of your business product and/or service meets both customer and internal requirements. These results may then contribute to improved efficiency, increased productivity, and less waste for your product and/or service delivery, which in turn maximizes your chances for profit unless you've incorrectly priced your product and/or service. As you can see, I suggest good employee morale may encourage continuous improvements, lead to business growth, generate more jobs, and eventually lead to maximum job security for everyone.

On the other hand, I also advise that bad employee morale may eventually lead to exactly the opposite results of good employee morale. Bad employee morale may cause people not to care about what they do, how they do it, and when they do it. Bad employee morale may lead to accidents, poor product and/or service quality, and late deliveries which then may result in upset customers, suppliers and, eventually, lost sales. These results, in turn, may lead to further employee morale declines—it's a vicious cycle that may continue until its eventual end when your business fails and closes.

So, how do you know, determine, or perhaps measure your employee morale? Personally, I have developed a keen sense of employee morale through several decades of experiences leading, interacting and working with, and observing many types of people in numerous different situations and work environments. I suggest there are informal ways to quickly and accurately assess the overall employee morale of your organization at any given moment provided you know what to look for. Perhaps you may consider implementing regular employee surveys as a more formal method to measure your overall employee morale. Employee surveys may be very useful to confirm any challenges and identify any underlying issues due to their anonymous nature where employees may express their appreciations and concerns without usual fear of potential retaliation(s). I recommend you consider implementing an employee survey strategy as long as your employees are sincere with their answers and you and your management team genuinely implement corrective actions to address any legitimate concerns.

Any formal or informal employee survey may identify what I recommend may be at least two "giant killers" of good employee morale: politics and bureaucracy. Politics and bureaucracy seem to be inherent in any group of people during any endeavour because there always seems to be a person(s) who desires the benefits of hard work and contribution but prefers to let others do all or most of the work. I recommend you, as the business leader, need to constantly monitor and reduce bureaucracy and politics at every opportunity, regardless of why or how they may exist within your organization at the moment. I also recommend you consider terminating the employment of anyone who seems to be more interested in politics and bureaucracy than in contributing to the success of their co-workers, your customers, suppliers, and your business success.

Building good employee morale may seem like a slow process requiring consistent efforts and multiple strategies to achieve and then maintain. You may need to spend months and years to consistently build good employee morale, while a single significant negative incident may suddenly diminish and/or completely destroy it in a moment's notice. Why? Employee morale can be thought of as the state of the relationship not only between you as the business leader and your employees, but also amongst your employees themselves. Even if you carefully ensure your business does not negatively affect any employee, good luck trying to manage or control relationships between people themselves. I advise you quickly assess the significance of, and appropriately address, any negative incident that may affect your overall employee morale.

Since employee morale can be thought of not only as the state of the relationship between you, as the business leader, and your employees, but also among your employees themselves, I suggest strategies to improve employee morale are very similar/identical to those used for any relationship. First and foremost, I recommend you always be open and honest while building trust with your employees. A second requirement for good employee morale is to demonstrate respect for your employees in every decision and action. I suggest there are very few things that people crave and demand more than respect. Another important aspect of any good relationship is to sincerely listen to your employees' ideas, including complaints and criticisms, and then do something(s) constructive to address any legitimate issue(s). I suggest it is more beneficial for you and your business that you hear firsthand an employee's idea and criticism rather than perhaps suffer the negative consequences of not doing so.

Another very important requirement for good employee morale is to always act with integrity, e.g. always deliver on all of your commitments. If you have any doubt(s) that you may not be able to deliver on any commitment(s), I suggest you consider not pledging to that commitment(s) at the moment. Instead, I recommend you consider committing to investigating an idea(s) and then promise to get back to the concerned employee(s)—and then actually do get back to them sooner than you promised, if possible.

A final element for good employee morale or any good relationship is to regularly recognize and show appreciation for your employees and their work—I will expand on this subject in the next section.

Employee Recognition

Recognition is a basic human need because we are all social by nature. Here is one piece of advice I have about recognition: be sincere. Any person or group of people may quickly sense and be offended when you are not genuinely sincere with your recognition. I also recommend you do not misinterpret other people's initial skepticism as you begin or continue to genuinely recognize their ideas, decisions, behaviours, and/or actions. When done sincerely and well, I suggest recognizing your people will also make you feel better too. And I also suggest you do not limit your recognition of others to only your employees—you should also recognize and show appreciation for your family, friends, and others on a regular basis.

There are many ways to recognize and show appreciation for your employees, some of which I have already discussed in the previous employee morale section. Sincerely listening to people, showing them respect, and always acting with integrity will go a long way to recognize and show appreciation for your employees as people and their contribution to your business. Depending on how many employees you have and how often you have a chance to see them, I recommend a simple act of saying "hello" to as many people as possible, once every day or so. I suggest investing time to stop by where they work or when they are on their way back to their work station, to get to know them, ask them how they are doing, and perhaps how their family and friends are doing, as appropriate. Your recognition could range from a wave of hand from a distance to a more lengthy and casual conversation. I suggest these actions virtually cost nothing financially or time-wise, but go a long way to foster harmonious relationships and improve employee morale.

As the overall business leader, I also suggest you consider recognizing peoples' birthdays by personally signing and giving birthday cards to all your employees on a monthly basis. I recommend you complete, sign, and deliver birthday cards personally to each employee at work, versus sending them to your employees' homes, to maximize this strategy's intended value, effects, and results. Your personal delivery of birthday cards offers you a chance to genuinely and personally get to know each and every employee, provides you an opportunity to recognize your employee on one of their special days, and allows you to speak with your employee on a one to one basis. But I also caution you to avoid any conversations about work or the business at this time. If your employee raises any work issue(s), I suggest you try to direct the conversation away from work to avoid any criticism that this act may be one of your ways to unofficially "get information from people." Some of your employees may initially be skeptical about your motives, especially if you are not sincere and/or your employees are experiencing this simple act of recognition for the first time. Trust me, after your first month, most of your employees may be looking forward to their turn to speak with the *big boss*. And don't be surprised if your employees remind you if you are late or perhaps skip this practice of recognition one month. I recommend you complete employee birthday cards on the first day of every month, and place them in their own envelope addressed to the person with their birthday month and day (never the year for privacy reasons) discretely written on the back or a front corner to remind you of their specific special day . I also advise you distribute birthday cards as soon as possible at the beginning of each month to acknowledge those birthdays occurring in the month's first few days. You may also consider recognizing employee birthdays by giving people the day off with pay or by providing a birthday cake to all employees on a monthly basis to acknowledge birthdays occurring that month.

Recognizing and celebrating hiring date anniversaries or seniority is another opportunity to acknowledge and recognize your employees' contribution to your business. For example, you can post special one-page letters, give out balloons, or provide cake for all employees to recognize peoples' seniority dates within any given month. Similar to birthdays, you can personally distribute a congratulatory card and/or recognize employees in front of everyone during monthly communication meetings. On special milestone work anniversaries, you may offer additional recognition and appreciation by taking employees out for lunch, giving them a nicely framed certificate/award, offering additional vacation days, or a gift(s). I caution you, though, to avoid any temptation to give out a gold watch—that's so "yesterday" in my opinion. Some people may appreciate cash, so I suggest you consider writing and presenting them a cheque in an amount that may not be lavish but large enough to be sincere. I also recommend you take a picture of you presenting certificates, cheques, and gifts to employees, post them on your bulletin boards, and include them in newsletters, as appropriate.

An employee's retirement is another occasion to recognize their contribution to your business. When an employee confirms they will retire, I recommend you offer and ask for their permission to publicly acknowledge them because you may find on occasion an employee that does not prefer any public recognition. That's fine, and I suggest you respect your employee's wishes in this matter. Similar to recognizing employees' seniority, you may do nothing or *go all out* depending on the circumstances of a person's retirement and their personal preferences. Whenever you arrange an onsite catered lunch or perhaps an offsite dinner, I recommend you also invite the retiring employee's family, give a speech about the person and their contributions to your business, let others offer their thoughts, and, of course, permit your retiring employee to speak and thank everyone as well.

There may be other occasions and ways to recognize an individual employee(s) who has achieved a milestone and/or major business objective. For example, you may offer to pay for an employee's dinner with their partner after they have completed an important business project. In this case, I advise you may need to remind your employee that they and their partner have dinner at a fancy restaurant that they may not usually go to on their own to ensure the occasion provides extra significance for them.

You can be creative and make your recognition extra fun, especially when acknowledging the achievements of a small group of employees. Let me demonstrate with a personal example. Soon after I assumed responsibility for a production process and its employees, I confirmed we suffered from regular customer quality issues. During our first employee team meeting, I raised the importance of improving our product quality after which an employee asked, "What's in it for us?" While resisting the temptation to lecture this person, I flippantly answered that "for every month we achieve zero rejects at the customer, we all eat cake!" Everyone laughed as I successfully diffused what could have been a potentially confrontational discussion. Over the next several weeks, we worked to eliminate and prevent any potential root cause that may have contributed to a faulty part(s) being manufactured and shipped to our customer. Soon after we achieved our first *reject-free* month, I ordered a large cake from a local bakery in the shape of a zero and personally served it to all my team members in the lunch room as dessert during their lunch break. Naturally, plant employees in the other production process teams also wanted cake. But by now they knew the rule: cake is served only when we all work together to ensure our production process manufactures and ships zero rejected parts to our customer(s) for the previous month. Guess what happened? We began achieving zero reject production over successive months, and many employees were eating cake once a month. I recall one employee jokingly asking if they may gain weight after eating so much cake. I jokingly replied, "I'm not sure. But the more cake you eat, the harder you'll need to work to burn off all those calories!"

As important as recognizing individuals and small groups of employees is to your business, I also suggest it is necessary to acknowledge all your employees as a group. Popular company employee recognition ideas include annual employee holiday parties (perhaps one party for your employees and a second party for them and their children) and summer picnics. You may also consider providing free tickets to a local amusement park or sports events so your employees and their families may attend at their own leisure, or have an employee picnic at that same amusement park. Golf tournaments may also be popular with your employees and a great way to show your appreciation for their contributions to your business. Typically, a good dinner and draw prizes following your day of playing golf are additional ways to recognize your employees. For each or some of these group events, you can ask suppliers or customers to donate prizes and/or you can also purchase prizes that will be raffled away. I encourage you to consider holding these group employee recognition and appreciation events since they are an excellent way to involve, appreciate, and thank your employees' family members and to recognize them for their sacrifices when your employees take extra time away from their families to work in your business.

Types of People at Work

I suggest your business can be considered a group of people that can be divided into three groups: *stars, workers,* and *rotten apples.* I recommend that you, as a business leader, need to support each of your employees to contribute at their optimum performance level once you've recognized their primary personality and behaviour. I also advise that some of your employees are not always stagnant in their current category, that sometimes an employee may transform themselves from a *worker* to a *star,* or to a *rotten apple,* or vice versa. I also suggest some people may act out different predominant personalities in different arenas of their life. I recommend that you as a prudent business leader should always notice these sometimes subtle personality changes that a single or small group of employees may undergo as you always treat your employees fairly. An effective leader will recognize the need to lead, manage, coach, and support each of these three types of personalities in slightly different and subtle ways to achieve overall business goals.

Stars are those employees who shine throughout your business and are critical to its success. Every team and organization, whether in sports, in a family, or in your business, has *stars,* and their numbers may seem to be too few at times. You may have heard versions of Pareto's Principle that 80% of results are generated by 20% of the people/efforts/tasks/activities—I suggest this statement is true. Your *star* employees typically thrive on challenges, change, a variety of tasks, on making a difference, and are self-starters—just tell them what needs to be done and they will get it done, and sometimes more. Your *star* employees are your *go to* people, especially when your business is in a crisis. But I suggest working with *stars* may come with issues as well, similar to a double-edged sword. I advise the challenge with your *star* employees is that you need to constantly quench their thirst for variety and challenges, and sometimes there may be only so many crises, challenges, or variety of tasks to go around in your business. As much as you may admire and wish at times you had more *stars* in your business, I suggest having too many *star* employees can also be a challenge. The reason for this is that *star* employees may eventually turn on each other and/or leave your business altogether in search of more challenges. Therefore, I caution you may need to be careful about how many *star* employees you can keep while running your business smoothly. And even if a *star* employee leaves, hopefully you and your business will have a remaining person(s) who will assume that *star* employee role.

Workers are the majority of your employees and I suggest you may be very thankful for that fact. There is nothing wrong with being a *worker* or having a lot of *workers* in your business. Your *worker* employees are those who come to work every day, want to be heard, recognized, get along with everyone else, contribute, be paid, and then go home. As I've already stated, some people may be a *star*, *worker*, or *rotten apple* in one life arena and another personality in other areas of life. Since *workers* may describe the majority of people in your organization, I recommend you always consider that fact when designing and implementing your business policies and practices. Your *worker* employees' needs may affect your business operations at times. For example, if the majority of your *worker* employees share a common tradition(s) or holiday(s), I advise you should not be surprised if some or many of them schedule some time off during regular business hours, once or several times a year to acknowledge that common tradition(s) or holiday(s). In such cases, I recommend you may consider adjusting your operations schedule(s) once or several times a year to recognize your employees' tradition(s) or holiday(s) outside of work. In turn, I suggest you and your business will benefit many times over with increased employee morale as you demonstrate respect for your employees' traditions and/or holidays outside of work.

Rotten apples—there seems to be that one or few people in every business, family, sports team, and any organization that just seem to want to ruin it for everyone else. At times you may wonder how your business ended up with such a *rotten apple* employee(s). Since I assume you nor anyone else intentionally hired a *rotten apple*, I suggest that most *rotten apples* actually reveal themselves and/or develop after they've been hired to work in your business.

I caution you not to conclude that an employee may be a *rotten apple* if they are outspoken, who may seem to "volunteer" their opinion in a one on one conversation, or who may intentionally or inadvertently challenge and/or embarrass you and/or your idea(s) in front of a group of people. I suggest you consider employees who exhibit these behaviours may be *stars in disguise*—people who at least have the courage to voice their and perhaps others' opinions. I advise you to consider your *stars in disguise* employees may come up with solutions to challenges and in fact contribute to your business's success. I also suggest your *stars in disguise* employees may be valuable to your business as long as they can be managed. If a *star in disguise* employee does inadvertently "cross the line," that's when I recommend you must provide them immediate feedback that they have gone too far, or else you may be in danger of creating a *rotten apple* employee.

When you conclude that you truly have a *rotten apple* employee, I recommend you first speak with them, find out what's going on, and see if you can help them transition to a *worker, star in disguise,* or even a *star* employee. If this transformation does not occur within a reasonable period of time, I then recommend you may have no other choice but to terminate their employment as soon as possible. I suggest a *rotten apple* employee's attitude, behaviour, and presence in your business may be thought of as a cancer that may spread and affect your other employees if left untreated. After a *rotten apple* employee's departure, I suggest the resulting improvements in remaining employees' morale and productivity will reward you and the business many times over. It may be a case of business short term pain for long term gain, but I advise it may be well worth it. And do you know the best way to avoid *rotten apple* employees? Don't hire them in the first place.

I suggest there is another way to classify your employees into two groups: influencers and non-influencers. You will find there always seems to be those few influencers directing the opinions of the remaining majority non-influencers in your business, every organization, and every group of people. Similar to some of your *star* employees, some *traditional influencers* may be those employees who are in positions of traditional leadership and authority. And similar to *star in disguise* employees, your business may also have influencers in disguise employees who may not occupy a traditional position of leadership and authority. Your *influencers in disguise* employees may also not be as outspoken as *stars in disguise*, but they do influence your other employees' opinions and behaviours. Once you confirm the identity(ies) of your influencer and non-influencer employees, I suggest you may more effectively plan how, what, and when you communicate certain issues and their intended effect(s) within your business.

When Times Get Tough

So, your business may not be going as well as it could be, and your sales may be "soft". Perhaps at least most of your employees may still be busy producing and delivering your business product(s) and/or service(s) for now. You may also have some employees temporarily not working much at times. One of the first actions some business leaders consider in this scenario is to consider laying off some employees. Why? Because some business leaders (and/or their financial advisors) look upon their payroll as one of their largest expenses (and that may be valid be depending on their cost structure) and laying off employees is one of the simplest, easiest, and immediate ways to reduce expenses. In reality, and as discussed in my other book *Charge Up Your Business!: 27 Ways to Boost Profits* (www.chargeupyourbusinessbook.com), your labour costs (depending on your overall cost structure) may actually be pale in comparison to your material and overhead costs (as a percentage of your sales) that may be just as simple and easy to temporarily curtail until your business finances improve. I suggest it may be considered hypocritical that some business leaders "preach" that that their employees are their number one asset, but then do not hesitate to lay them off at the first sign(s) of any business downturn. I suggest your decision to lay off any employees, even temporarily, may have disastrous consequences to your business costs and growth.

I suggest you consider there are several value added activities your employees can perform as alternatives to suffering layoffs until customer demands return to more traditional levels, assuming your business can sustain your employees for some reasonable period of time. Your employees can complete workplace organization, preventative, and other inventory accuracy activities, and/or can undergo required health and safety, environment, quality, and other required trainings. Your employees can also contribute to various continuous improvement, research and development projects, and/or can book some time off as vacations. Depending on your situation, your business may be eligible to participate in government workshare programs, or your employees may volunteer to reduce their individual hours and pay in return to avoiding any layoffs. You may also ask your employees for their feedback and consideration of these or any other alternatives to any layoff(s); you may find your employees very receptive to some of these ideas and have others of their own.

Before laying off any employee(s), even temporarily, I recommend you consider all the potential ramifications and consequences to your business in the short, medium, and long terms, in addition to the short-term financial savings. Consider, for example, the effect on the morale of your remaining employees, knowing their friends/co-workers are at home without pay while they are still at work; some of your remaining employees may even feel guilty that they are still working. Other remaining employees may think the wrong people were sent home and others undeservedly remain at work and are still being paid. I propose there may be very real costs and/or profit reductions associated with lower employee morale, and perhaps lower quality and delivery performances following an employee layoff. And even if/when you bring back your laid-off employees, I suggest all your employees may be on edge or apprehensive on a regular basis, wondering when the next layoff may occur, especially if sales slow down again for any period of time. Layoff rumours may start every time employees see that everyone is not always busy for whatever reason(s), and then you need to spend time managing those rumours unless you want them to cause additional issues for your business.

I acknowledge and understand that laying off an employee(s) may be necessary for your current and particular business situation—I empathize with you. I recommend you, as do I, consider laying off any employee(s) as a last resort and to avoid this action if you can find a way(s) to do so without significantly affecting your business. I suggest your employees will remember your support and decision "to keep everyone" and will reward you and your business with their support, loyalty, and dedication, especially whenever you and your business may be in need of their extraordinary support.

For More Information and Advice

Please contact us at www.chargeupyourpeoplebook.com and/or www.gbicego.com if you would like more information and advice for your people challenges such as how to lead and work with people, employee morale, employee recognition, types of people at work, what to do when times get tough, and/or any other challenges—we are here to help.

CHAPTER 4

YOUR COMMUNICATIONS

Communications

Many people think the purpose of communication is to transfer an idea(s) or knowledge from one individual to another or between groups of people. In many ways, this is true and is a basic purpose of all communication. An additional, more *senior*, purpose of communications is to create a relationship between individuals and/or groups of people. Since communication is an important part of any relationship foundation, I recommend your business leadership effectiveness is mainly determined by your communications skills.

Communication methods between people have been invented throughout the millennia. The most common communication method is the spoken word reflected by the thousands of languages and their dialects. We also have the written word—each major language in the world consists of hundreds of thousands of words. The spoken and written word became our two major means of communication between people until the recent century when other means of communication and delivering our ideas were invented. For example, consider the printed word (in forms such as books, newspapers, and magazines), sign language, braille, radio, television, audio tapes, CDs, digital audio, videos, movies, the Internet, emails, and texting. Who knows what new communications methods will be invented in the near and/or not too distant future.

Despite the abundance of verbal communication, it is generally accepted that most communication between people has been determined to be non-verbal in nature. In fact, studies have concluded that over ninety percent of our communications are considered non-verbal, with the remaining less than ten percent believed to be verbal in nature. It is also generally accepted that most non-verbal communication consists of our body language and tone of voice. Consider how many facial expressions, body movements, postures, and gestures we all have. Also consider how many ways we can or cannot establish eye contact, how we can touch, and how much time and space we give each other during our communications. Even our clothing and how we present ourselves (e.g. personal hygiene) are considered forms of non-verbal communication.

With thousands of languages and dialects, hundreds of thousands of words, numerous non-verbal ways of communications unique to each individual at any given time, and the fact that people perceive and process information through their own personal mental filters, it may seem like a miracle at times when people understand each other at all. How many times have you concluded or suspected the cause(s) of an issue(s) between two people or groups of people may be attributed to a miscommunication(s)? How many misunderstandings, disagree-ments, and conflicts could have been avoided in the past, and may be avoided in the present and future, if the involved parties took or take the time to ensure there was or are no miscommunication(s) between them? As a business leader, I recommend what, how, when, and why you communicate anything may be critically important to your business success, since your employees, customers, and suppliers are constantly monitoring and studying every one of your decisions and actions.

Business communications can be classified as either formal or informal. Similar to verbal and non-verbal types of communications, I recommend both your formal and informal business communications skills are critical and required to deliver and emphasize your business values, priorities, and decisions. Let's expand upon some formal and informal business communication methods at your disposal.

Formal Communications

Formal business communications occur when you, as the business leader, communicate directly with people about an issue(s) at hand, typically at a predetermined date and time. Similar to verbal communications, formal communication methods may at first glance seem to be more prevalent within your business and may occur one-on-one between two people or within a group of people.

One-on-one communication between two individuals is the oldest and perhaps most common type of formal business communication. I recommend one-on-one communication is especially beneficial when you want to discuss an issue(s) that is or should be exclusive, private, and confidential between both parties. This may sound obvious, but how many times have you heard when a person inappropriately discusses an issue(s) with a group of people about another person who is not present in that group? I suggest you, as the business leader, may also prefer to use one-on-one communication to emphasize the importance of an issue(s) with a specific person. I also advise you use the one-on-one, face-to-face communication method for your most important discussions with other people. I also suggest, even with current social media alternatives, no other means of communication may be more powerful than a one-on-one, face-to-face conversation.

I recommend an important detail to remember in a one-on-one communication (especially when delegating a task or coming to an agreement) is to obtain confirmation that both parties understand what needs to be done, how, and by when. I propose this summary near the end of your one-on-one communication, either in verbal or written form, may provide both parties with a to-do list and reduce the chances of any misunderstandings. Although it may on occasion seem like a waste of time or just repeating what you've both already committed to earlier, this summary may be well worth the extra few seconds or minute to avoid any miscommunications and/or setting up false expectations.

A formal pre-scheduled meeting is perhaps the most common means of one-on-one communication within a group. Typically, there is a meeting leader presenting to a group of people, or groups of people, communicating with each other where each group typically has a group leader that speaks on behalf of their group. I suggest you consider, as I do, reducing as many formal pre-scheduled meetings as possible. Why? You may find some formal pre-scheduled meeting discussions tend to go off course, attendees seem not to accomplish what was set out to be done or anything at all, and run overtime, preventing some/all participants from attending other meetings or dealing with other more value-added business issues. I also suggest you consider holding, as I do, impromptu meetings where you assemble the necessary people, debate and discuss all possible solutions to an issue(s), ask for everyone's input, decide as the leader what next step(s) to implement, and then follow-up. I recommend you eliminate as many formal, scheduled non-value added meetings as possible, except employee communications meetings, since they may become a political arena for some employees to promote their own agendas and a bureaucratic obstacle to value added work that needs to be completed within your business.

If a formal pre-scheduled meeting is deemed necessary, I recommend they are conducted as infrequently and efficiently as possible. First of all, I advise all formal pre-scheduled meetings start on time no matter what; I suggest starting late just trains everyone that tardiness is acceptable. I also advise every formal pre-scheduled meeting have a meeting leader and/or facilitator, and that an agenda is designed and distributed well beforehand detailing the meeting start and end times, location, invited attendees, and items for discussions. I also recommend participants first discuss the agenda items only; new topics may or may not be briefly discussed depending on their relevance and the remaining time allotted for the meeting. I advise you may also consider "parking" any unrelated topic raised during a meeting, i.e. make a note of the issue to at least acknowledge the person(s) who raised it, and then return to the original meeting agenda. I also recommend you assign a person as a meeting scribe to record the discussion highlights, decisions, delegated actions/tasks, and each task deadline date, allowing all attendees to fully participate in the meeting discussions. As a final note, I recommend the resulting meeting minutes be completed, reviewed, and distributed as soon as possible to allow the meeting attendees or others to complete their tasks and set business directions as required.

Employee communications meetings are one of the few formal pre-scheduled meetings I recommend you must always conduct on a regular basis (others are joint and safety committee, and sales and marketing meetings). I advise that regular employee communications meetings are a must since they help keep your employees informed about current business issues and provide you, as the business leader, an opportunity to gauge your overall employee morale. Although you may have (as have I) led some tough employee communications meetings, I suggest you may cause more issues for your business if you do not conduct regularly scheduled formal employee communications meetings. These meetings offer your employees an opportunity to question you and management about relevant issues while providing you an occasion to address those issues, and correct any rumours that may perforate without factual data. I also recommend you implement a standard employee communications meeting agenda to reinforce your business priorities such as safety, quality, production/throughput, costs, continuous improvement work team presentations, employee recognition, and any announcements.

Informal Communications

Most communications may be considered informal similar to the generally accepted understanding that most of our communications are non-verbal in nature. Informal communications occur between two individuals or between you and a group of people without any predetermined date, time, and/or agenda.

The form and place of an informal communication can vary from a spontaneous face-to-face conversation in a hallway, on the plant floor, in an office, away from a place of business altogether, or over a phone, to a written memo, letter, email, or text. I suggest most of your business communications as a leader is informal in nature and may also be considered more efficient to accomplish your own personal business objectives. For example, you may learn much more about a person, their character, thoughts, and opinions by just listening to them after they stop you for a conversation, even if that conversation is not work related. For an untrained person, such a conversation may be a waste of time, but I suggest they may provide you *nuggets* of information and a better insight into your overall business and the people involved within it.

Your customer's, suppliers', and employees' morale may also be considered another form of informal communication. You may have heard that the *rumour mill* is typically the best maintained piece of equipment in any business and/or market place. I strongly recommend you, as the business leader, to listen or watch for clues of any changes in your customer's, suppliers', or employees' morale. I suggest you may sense this pulse or vibe by watching how people interact with each other and/or with you, how they move, if they are smiling or sad, talkative or quiet. Your sense of overall customer, supplier, and employee morale may contain subtle but very accurate clues of how your business is performing and how it will do so in the near future.

Communication Rules

As already mentioned, I suggest the purpose of communications is to transfer data and/or knowledge and create relationships with other people. I have listed below some advice, ideas for improvement, rules, and suggested practices for your verbal and non-verbal, and formal and informal communication methods as a business leader.

I recommend you positively praise a person in public while constructively criticizing them in private. There may be no other act that can damage and/or destroy a relationship as effectively and quickly than negatively criticizing someone in public to other people, with or without their presence. You must be prepared to accept the consequences of a potentially damaged relationship with anyone who you negatively criticize in public. There are advantage(s) though to using someone's action(s) and/or behaviour(s) in public as an example for improvement(s). In this case, I strongly recommend you do not directly or indirectly reveal that person's identity and clearly distinguish between the person and their actions and/or behaviors. On the other hand, and unless a person may be embarrassed and/or negatively affected, I suggest you share any success story about an individual's or group's achievement(s) with as many other people as appropriate. This action accomplishes three objectives: 1. it acknowledges the person and/or group for their achievement(s), 2. it encourages the group and/or group to repeat a similar or better performance/result(s), and 3. it sets an example for other individuals and groups to achieve similar or better results.

Related to my point above, I recommend you always focus on a person's behaviours and actions and never on any person themselves. Sure, a person's behaviour(s) and/or action(s) may not be acceptable, and may cause anger and/or frustration. I advise you consider that a person's behaviour(s) and/or action(s) may not always define who that person genuinely is at times. Even though this statement may sound contradictory, as a prudent leader I suggest you consider asking yourself if a person's specific behaviour(s) and/or action(s) makes sense or is normal for that individual. If your answer is "no," I suggest you may need to further investigate what is really going on and/or causing a person's particular behaviour(s) and/or action(s).

Before accusing anyone of anything, I strongly advise you communicate your concern in the form of a general non-offensive question rather than a specific accusatory statement. For example, if you suspect someone may have stolen or taken an item, I advise you pose a more general non-offensive question such as "Do you know what may have happened to this item?" versus a more specific accusatory statement such as, "Why or did you take this item?" I suggest a more general non-accusatory question combined with their reply (with both verbal and non-verbal clues) will better help you to determine a genuine answer without potentially offending the other person(s). Your relationship with that other person(s) may suffer permanent damage if your assumption expressed as an initial specific accusatory statement eventually turned out to be incorrect.

I caution you that electronic and digital means of communications such as emails, texts, blogs, videos, and pictures may be more *permanent* than ink. I advise you to take a deep breath, pause, or wait to reconsider if you should reply to a frustrating email and/or text in a similar manner, or if you should reply at all at times. I offer this same advice when you may be face-to-face with another person in a frustrating conversation. You may be considering the potential advantages and disadvantages of not replying at all; perhaps a *non-reply* may effectively terminate the on-going issue but may also be considered unprofessional. I am not suggesting you should back down from any debate and from making any of your arguments, but to avoid what may be considered aggressive and unprofessional behaviour in your communications. I recommend you always consider replying to every (non-spam) email and text in a professional and courteous manner, even if the other person(s) is being belligerent and unfair.

Unprofessional and belligerent email and text behaviours include typing words with all capital letters, using bold fonts, and/or colours such as red—these are examples of bad email/text etiquette and may come back to *haunt* you, your business, and others for decades to come. I suggest you consider the following strategy, as I do, when you feel like responding to an email in an angry or frustrated manner: 1. most important, initially delete all recipients in the reply email To line to avoid inadvertently sending your reply, 2. reply as you feel at the moment to *let it all out*, and 3. take some time to reflect upon your original answer, modify, and send it with a more cooperative tone. I suggest this strategy may permit you to let out your frustrations and anger, at least in written form, and enable you to *feel better* and less frustrated and/or angry. I also advise this approach provides you an opportunity to reassess a particular situation, may prevent any further relationship damage at least on your part, and allows you to reply in a more professional manner.

When using a cell phone, I suggest you always be aware of and adjust your cell phone volume depending upon your surroundings. You may have experienced the annoyance of loud cell phone rings or alerts when you have been enjoying a conversation, attending a movie, training, or being in a place of worship. To avoid such unnecessary disruptions and annoyances, I suggest you at least switch all electronic devices to vibrate or silent mode, or perhaps shut them off as appropriate—doing so demonstrates your respect for the other individuals' enjoyment and peace of mind. Likewise, I recommend you immediately notify anyone who is on your speaker phone at the beginning of a conversation and to respect any request they be removed from speaker phone.

As a business leader, I recommend you always be transparent about your intentions and expectations when communicating with your employees, customers, suppliers, and anyone else for that matter. I advise you always speak clearly and with posture to verbally and non-verbally demonstrate your authority and expertise. At the same time, I suggest you always communicate in a straightforward, honest manner and with integrity. No one likes anyone who "beats around the bush," especially when delivering bad news.

How should you deliver news that may be considered bad and/or good? I suggest what you consider to be *good* or *bad* news may not apply to others. Similar to the concept of data neutrality, news can be at times considered good and/or bad, depending upon on each person's perspective(s). For example, you may consider that informing a person that their employment is being terminated may be perceived as bad news by them. But you may be surprised; the other person may consider this news to be good, since they will now have an opportunity to pursue other priorities and/or may have been unhappy in their role(s) within your business anyway.

What if you need to communicate what may be considered both good and bad news? Which one do you deliver first? The answer to this question depends on your intent. You may consider to first deliver the good news, depending on your audience's collective mood and/or expectation. But if you are unsure, I recommend you (as I do) deliver the bad news first, followed by the good news at the end of your communication. I recommend you deliver your bad news first and your good news second, for two reasons: 1. I suggest people typically remember and focus on the last major discussion point of your communications, so why not let it be *good versus bad,* and 2. considering the previous reason, I suggest your audience may more likely remember your entire communications as positive and beneficial.

I also recommend you are timely with all your communications. For example, reply to emails, texts, phone calls, and messages as soon as possible. Unless under extenuating circumstances, I suggest the timeliness of your reply(ies) demonstrates how much you value your relationship and respect the other person. I also recommend you arrive early for meetings and complete other commitments early; trying to be *on time* rarely works. As a business leader, I suggest you set the tone and levels of expectations for the rest of your business; you must always be mindful of what example(s) you are setting for everyone else. If you expect to arrive late for a meeting, I advise you notify the other party(ies) as early as possible to demonstrate your respect for their time and to provide them an opportunity to work on other priorities as they wait for your arrival. I suggest that *not* advising anyone if you know you will be late for a meeting or a commitment deadline, is a sure way to damage a relationship, unless that is your intention. If it is your goal to modify or end a relationship, I suggest you find another means of communication to accomplish your objective(s).

At times, you may need to find alternate means of communications if you find the current one is ineffective. This statement may seem like common sense, but how many times have you listened to someone complain that their associate "never answers the phone" but they continue to try calling them on their phone! Another example: ever notice that some people seem to rarely reply to a telephone call or voice message but quickly reply to an email or even faster to a text? The opposite may also be true. For example, you may find that emailing or texting someone is a waste of your time and may damage your relationship, because that person only believes in one-on-one communication, either face-to-face or via phone. In the end, I recommend you determine and then consistently use whatever means of communications works best between you and your audience.

Similar to the above practice, I also recommend you consider to adapting what, how, and when to deliver your message(s) to your audience based on who they are and their objectives they wish to achieve by receiving your message(s). I suggest your communications *stay on topic* when delivering your message(s) and perhaps avoid using generally unknown words unless you define those words during your communication. I also recommend you avoid *speaking above* and/or *speaking below* your audience, since either style is considered offensive to most people who may not receive your intended message(s).

I advise you avoid using useless words or expressions in your statements such as *um, you know,* and *ah.* Many people are not consciously aware of these "dead" words in their communications, and even worse many other people do not notice them either. Unfortunately, for many people, other individuals may judge them by their vocabulary and the use or absence of useless "dead" words such as *um* or *ah.*

I also suggest you, as a business leader, may consider to listen more to what other people say rather than try to speak more than they do; there may be a reason(s) why we are equipped with two ears and one mouth. This communication strategy may permit you to learn and gain more insights about another person, a group, or a situation. It is generally accepted that conscious processing of information or learning stops once you begin to speak. I also recommend you consider remaining silent if and/or when you feel you have nothing valuable to say and/or nothing "good" to say. I suggest you may consider adhering to the phrase *silence is golden* and avoid the temptation to fill any conversation void with meaningless chatter.

As the business leader, I recommend you communicate sooner rather than later and on a regular basis. You may also consider adapting your words and/or your communications methods to emphasize major themes or ideas. I suggest you also tell people as much as you know at the moment, and commit to providing more information as it becomes available. On some occasions, you may need to consider using some discretion of what you say with whom, especially if such information may reflect badly on other people and/or may create some sort of advantage for some people. I suggest discretely sharing confidential information may build trust between you and other people, but I also advise you remain constantly aware if such confidential information eventually *leaks out.* If so, I recommend you may need to reconsider with whom you share confidential information.

When your business is in the midst of a crisis, as the business leader I recommend that you always take command of the situation and remain calm in your demeanour, while at the same time not being afraid to "shout orders." Typically, when other people are overwhelmed during a crisis, I suggest you, as the business leader, must quickly evaluate with an open mind what is happening and why. I advise you formulate a plan(s) by consulting with others, if feasible, to resolve the crisis as soon as possible, assign tasks to others, and then follow-up on those tasks. I also suggest it may not be important that you anticipate every detail of your crisis action plan(s) at first, but rather that you start acting on and improving the situation as soon as possible. You can adjust your plan(s) and actions accordingly as additional information and results reveal themselves through the crisis.

And, finally, I recommend you always practise what many refer to as the *golden rule*: treat others as you would like to be treated. I also advise you always say *please* and *thank you*. Although practising the golden rule may seem challenging, and saying please and thank you may sound elementary at times, I recommend you always communicate in a courteous and professional manner within and outside your business activities. And regardless if others may not practice communications rules presented in this section, I recommend you do so as a business leader. Leading by example is a *price* of leadership in my opinion.

For More Information and Advice

Please contact us at www.chargeupyourpeoplebook.com and/or www.gbicego.com if you would like more information and advice for your communication challenges such as communications in general, formal communications, informal communications, communications rules and/or any other challenges— we are here to help.

CHAPTER 5

HUMAN RESOURCES – PART I

Introduction to Human Resources

In previous chapters, I suggested your employees are your most important business asset, how to lead and work with your people, and how to effectively communicate with them. I suggest treating your employees well is not only *the right thing to do* and shows your respect for them, but also allows them to contribute to your business and customers at their maximum performance. In this and the next two chapters, I offer a variety of required and practical human resources ideas and practices that will help you support the needs of your employees who will in turn support your customers and business.

At first, you may start your business by yourself with no employees— who knows, perhaps that's how you prefer to run your business. Before starting to expand your new business or growing an existing one by adding employees, I recommend you first create a human resources plan detailing how many people your business needs and what qualifications they require to complete their duties. I also recommend using at least two tools to create your human resources plan: an organization chart and job descriptions.

You may question the benefits and disadvantages of an organization chart and/or job descriptions, and the details/extent to which you develop either one or both for your business. On one hand, your organization chart and job descriptions may provide your employees with structure and sets of expectations and guidelines. On the other hand, you may be concerned an organization chart and job descriptions may constrict your employees' creativity and/or be used as a reason(s) to avoid completing certain tasks. In the end, I recommend you establish and effectively use your organization chart and job descriptions as part of your human resources plan—even if you may hire just one employee.

Organization Chart

Your business organization chart may be designed before or simultaneously while developing your business job descriptions. The purposes of your organization chart is to provide a structure for your business and establish relationship(s) between each position and the people who occupy them. The vast majority of business organization charts are designed with a *top-down* structure, although I have also seen a *straight line* structure.

The traditional business organization chart structure is a top-down structure, popularized by the military with the general position on top, subordinate officer positions beneath the top level, such as colonel and major, all the way to the enlisted positions at the bottom. In business terms, the chief executive officer and/or president position is on top, followed by each vice president and management position, all the way to each line employee position at the bottom. I recommend you optimize the number of management levels in your organization while balancing your business objectives, operations efficiencies, and costs.

Another business organization chart structure is a flatter straight line style showing very few management levels. A flatter organization chart structure typically shows a straight line *core process* linking your business departments or functions and how they collectively produce and deliver your company product and/or service. Customer expectations can be located at both ends to reinforce the philosophy that your business, its operations, and processes start and finish with your customers' expectations, who are in turn supported by your business core process. Your direct or *line* employee positions are located at the top, directly underneath their respective departments or function areas supporting your core process. This positioning reinforces the concepts that their job is to directly support the business core process and their internal customer is the next step or people in your core business process. Your department or function manager/supervisor positions are then located underneath the direct or line employee positions to reinforce the concept that their job is to support their department *line* employees.

Personally, I have seen and used both these business organization structures, and sometimes hybrids where senior leadership positions are located above the straight line business core process. When using the flatter straight line business organization chart structure, you may consider placing your position at the very bottom to reinforce the concept that it is your responsibility to support and/or direct your senior leadership employees and that your entire organization can pivot on your decisions and actions. In turn, your senior leadership employees' main responsibility is to support their department leaders and/or direct or *line* employees, and everyone collectively supports your business core process that begins and ends with your customers' expectations. I recommend you select and use whatever organization chart structure makes sense for you and your company, and supports your business objectives.

At times it may seem to make sense and be convenient that a single and/or group of positions report(s) to more than one other position(s); this situation may be displayed on an organization chart with a dashed line between such positions. I recommend you consider avoiding designing or setting up an employee position to report to more than another single employee position(s), directly or indirectly—in my opinion, you may be setting up that employee or group of employees for failure. I suggest this approach may result in confusion and frustrations, and perhaps create more problems for your business than you think you may be resolving by attempting to implement such a strategy.

Job Descriptions

Job descriptions document the purpose(s), minimum expectations, responsibilities, and qualifications for each position within your business organization chart and are an excellent tool to help you achieve your hiring objectives. You may also utilize job descriptions as a strategy to identify and dismiss potential employee candidates who may not be qualified and/or prepared to perform all job responsibilities before or during your interview process. Another advantage of designing and using job descriptions is they eliminate any excuses some potential or current employee(s) may use to initially not complete a task(s) that may not be specifically detailed in their job description (more on how to accomplish this below).

You may find employees at times may try to use current job descriptions to limit what they do when working in your business by making statements such as, "It's not my job," or "It's not in my job description." Although you (as do I) may find such statements frustrating, on occasion such statements may be valid since your employee may not be sufficiently trained and/or have the experience to complete a particular task(s). In that case, I recommend you ensure your employee obtains the required training and/or experience before starting the task(s) in question. To counteract any phoney "It's not my job and/or department" claim, especially if your employee has sufficient training and/or experience, I recommend the last line in the responsibilities section of every job description states something like: "Any other responsibilities assigned by you (insert your position or the most senior leadership position here) and/or their designate."

I also recommend all your business job descriptions be constructed with a common format. Every job description should contain the job title, position to which this position reports to, if it is a full or part time position, compensation type (salary or hourly), location (address) of work, any amount of travel required, and the job description revision date. Every job description should also include the position's list of duties and responsibilities (including the last "and/or any other responsibilities..." line item), working relationships, required minimum skills and experience, description of the work environment, and any other suitable items. Finally, every job description should include an acknowledgement section where the employee agrees they have reviewed, had an opportunity(ies) to ask questions, and agrees the job description forms part of their employment contract with your company. I suggest you place one signed copy of the employee's signed job description in their personnel file and give another copy to the employee.

Designing Your Team

I propose one of your most important and critical business decisions is who you will hire as your employees to help achieve your company's goals—I cannot stress enough how important your hiring decisions are for your business success. Your employees have an enormous potential to make or break your business success; therefore, I recommend you always choose your employees wisely.

Many business leaders may consider two strategies when looking to employ people: employees should share similar characteristics, behaviours, and opinions with them and each other, or they should have different attributes with them and each other. On one hand, you may be attempting to ensure everyone gets along so you can avoid potential issues that may distract you from other business priorities. On the other hand, you may be considering a strategy to hire people whose strengths compensate for your business's current weaknesses. I recommend you consider pursuing the latter strategy thus avoiding to hire too many people who are *similar* to you and others in your business. Let me explain with a personal experience.

I and other senior business leaders attended a personality and leadership training where we determined each other's work leadership styles represented by colours. We learned that everyone has a mixture of traits associated with each colour, and each person has a colour combination representing some traits being more predominant than others. After we determined and shared our work leadership profiles, the trainer led us through group exercises. In the first exercise, we were separated into groups according to our dominant colour and given the task to generate a solution(s) for a particular challenge. For the next hour, we all witnessed how each group either self-imploded or could not generate an effective solution(s) to that first challenge. In the second exercise, we were again separated into groups, but this time each group consisted of people with a combination of all dominant colours. We quickly realized how much easier it was to generate more effective discussions and potential solutions to the new challenge when we were assigned to groups that contained a variety of work personalities. We also witnessed and proved the results of each of the second exercise groups, and the overall combined result of the second groups were far better than in the first exercise.

I recommend all your employees must share your corporate values and goals, certain characteristics such as honesty and integrity, and be able to reasonably get along with others. I also recommend, as shown in the above real-life training exercise example, you should hire a mix or combination of employees whose diverse personalities, viewpoints, and opinions are different enough to stimulate beneficial debates and generate more and effective potential solutions to various business challenges. Your diverse group of employee personalities may also result in a more vibrant, flexible, and stronger business, better equipped to meet and/or exceed your customers' expectations.

Your Hiring Process

You may be considering what amount of *gut feeling* you should use when making a hiring decision or any other decision for that matter. You may have sat with or heard a successful business person state that they primarily use their gut feeling to make major business decisions. Some people may misinterpret such a statement as being that those people only use their gut feeling to make major decisions and that successful gut feelings typically are developed with extensive experiences. I recommend you consider making major business decisions, such as hiring, based on a *combination* of a decision matrix and using your gut feeling to confirm the results of your decision-matrix process.

Your hiring decision matrix process first starts with constructing a list of the job position's personal and technical skills, qualities, characteristics, and requirements, as well as determining the *weight* or contribution factor of each item. After every interview, you and/or the interviewer scores each candidate on each hiring matrix list item and multiplies each item score by its weight or contribution factor. Your third step is to sum up the weighted item scores to generate the total interview score for each candidate. I suggest this process typically narrows down the field of potential candidates to one or a few *short list* finalists that may be invited back for additional and perhaps more-in-depth interviews. As a final step, I suggest you consider using your gut feeling to confirm the final choice revealed by your hiring decision matrix process.

I recommend you reconsider your final hiring decision if there is a conflict between your gut feeling and your hiring decision matrix process result. Let me demonstrate with a personal experience. At one time, early in my career, I needed to fill a new position within my department. I designed the position job description, created my hiring decision matrix, conducted interviews, and completed evaluations for several candidates. My decision matrix process was pointing towards an individual that seemed most qualified, but my *gut feeling* told me they may not fit well into our company. After trying to *rejig* or revise the candidate scores within reason, I concluded this same individual was the best available person at the time, so I hired them despite not having a positive gut feeling. Guess what happened? Soon after this person began working with us, we experienced several minor issues; but with time, the sum of these minor issues developed into a major issue. While thinking about possible solutions to this challenge, this individual came into my office one day and announced their resignation. I was so relieved. Through this experience, I learned and recommend you seriously reconsider your hiring decision matrix process result if there is a conflict between your *gut feeling* and that result.

In another related hiring experience, later in my career, I recall interviewing and rejecting so many candidates for an important senior manager position that I spent several weeks to find a qualified individual who possessed the position's minimum requirements and qualifications, and who passed my final *gut feel confirmation test.* I used my hiring decision matrix to pre-qualify potential candidates on their personal and technical abilities, and then relied on my gut feeling to make my final selection. After many interviews, over several weeks, I almost hired on the spot a person who seemed to fit all the position's criteria and passed my *gut feel test* with flying colours; but I did not follow through on this strong impulse at the time in order to practice prudence with this important decision. Instead, I went home that night, "slept on it," and hired that individual the following morning— it was one of the best hiring decisions I've ever made.

I recommend you consider making your hiring decisions based slightly more on personal traits and organizational *fit* within your company than technical skills, unless you are hiring for a very technical position that has little or no interaction with other people. I advise you consider a 60% personal/40% technical score, even for more technical positions, because if a candidate demonstrates good personal traits such as getting along with others and corporate fit, I suggest they may most likely also possess the ability to learn whatever technical skills necessary to contribute to your business's overall success. There may be exceptions to this recommendation, especially when the successful candidate must have very technical and unique skills that may be rarely possessed by any individual. In such cases, I recommend you adjust your hiring decision matrix personal/technical percentage split as appropriate and whatever makes sense for your business.

As a final piece of hiring advice, I recommend you use an employment contract whenever you offer employment to anyone for several reasons. First and foremost, an employment contract may be used to outline the person's and job responsibilities, compensation, and other employment conditions. I also advise you refer to and attach a job description and acknowledgement form to every employment offer/contract. I also recommend you utilize an employment offer/contract to predetermine conditions for termination by either party such as severance and/or termination pay. Without such termination terms in an employment offer/contract, you and your business may be subject to common law cases in your jurisdiction— and you may not like those settlements. As with all contracts, I recommend you insert a clause that states that any contract item(s) that does not meet minimum legal requirements may be cancelled or separated from the contract but does not cancel the entire contract. I also strongly recommend you contact a legal professional who specializes in employment law within your business jurisdiction to develop template employment offers/contracts for every type of position within your company.

Your Interview Style

Your interview style can be as unique as your leadership style; you may possess characteristics associated with other common styles but, ultimately, each interview is unique because it occurs between two exclusive individuals. An interview can be a nerve-wracking experience for both interviewer and interviewee. Typically, some people think the interviewee may be on the spot to give a great first impression and the interviewer may "hold all the cards." That may seem to be true in some respects, but I suggest you consider another point of view. I suggest one of your main responsibilities as the interviewer is to attract the best possible people to your business rather than sifting through candidates to find a qualified person(s) for the available position(s). I advise you also consider this philosophy of attracting the best people possible because I am sure you agree *good people* are always hard to find.

There are a number of effective steps for an interviewer to prepare for an interview process. Your initial steps should be to design and review your position job description, hiring decision matrix, and list of candidate questions. I also suggest you review each candidate's resume, perhaps writing notes and questions about interesting points in them to be used as discussion points. You may consider asking standard interview questions—"What are your strengths?" "What are your weaknesses?" "Where do you see yourself in five years?" "Why did you leave that position?"—just to "break the ice" during the interview initial stages. But I also caution you that most candidates may have prepared answers to these *standard* interview questions. My advice is to consider minimizing the amount of time spent on standard interview questions unless you are seeking to fill a *standard position* with a *standard person*, if they exist.

I recommend you consider spending most of your interview time discussing open-ended questions rather than closed questions that may be replied with prepared, *yes* or *no* answers. As an experienced and skilled interviewer, I suggest you may receive more valued answers to standard interview questions scattered with open-ended questions throughout a conversation. I also suggest you may also find this *conversation interview technique* creates a more relaxed atmosphere, permitting both of you to learn more about each other versus the traditional higher-pressure list of standard questions interview method. You may consider preparing and showing a brief presentation at the beginning of each interview to show each candidate details about your company, your organization chart, and position job description. You may also find candidates tell you, as they have told me, they enjoyed this *conversation style* interview format. That's good news for you and your business since your conversation interview style may be another advantage that sets your company and the position apart from other opportunities candidates may be considering at that time.

Who Should Interview Whom and Where?

Depending on your hiring objectives, company size, and the type of position(s) available, you may design your hiring process where multiple people interview each candidate in stages at your facility, or perhaps you will exclusively interview all candidates on-site and/or at an off-site location(s). In the first case, I advise you to consider posting a job opportunity notice internally and interviewing any current and interested employee(s) eager to advance their career within your business. This strategy benefits both your employees and business since it allows them to advance their career growth, reduces any required training period, and demonstrates your commitment to providing advancement opportunities to your employees. In the latter case, your hiring objectives may include to employ an *outsider* that may not possess any current organizational paradigms and a high-energy drive to "shake things up" and improve progress to achieve your business objectives.

I recommend you involve and permit your other employees to interview candidates whenever possible and appropriate, at least the final few people on any candidate short list. How many times have you seen or heard of more experienced employees resigning from their position(s) because other newer employees joined a company? Unless this is your objective, I suggest that involving other current employees in the hiring process benefits your business by giving them a say as to who is hired, as well as offering them an opportunity to practice their interviewer skills. I suggest additional benefits include the fact that your current employees may confirm if potential candidates will *fit* into your corporate culture, and they may offer supplementary opinions and insights that you may not have considered in your own analyses.

Onboarding Checklist

So, you've completed your job description and hiring decision matrix, interviewed and considered your current employees' opinions of all candidates, made an employment offer, had the contract signed by your new employee, and confirmed their start date. Congratulations! On their new employee's first day, many companies just "throw them into the deep end to sink or swim." I suggest this practice may be one of the worst things any company can do to any new employee and to the rest of their current employees. Consider how most new employees, full of anticipation and excitement, may think and feel when they are "thrown into the deep end to sink or swim" on their first day. Consider how current employees may think and feel when a new person suddenly appears in their workplace without any notice. Both new and current employees may think and feel under-appreciated after a new employee starts with a company without any proper notice and/or introduction.

I suggest you consider the arrival of your new employee as a celebration reflected by designing and implementing an onboarding policy and procedure. Your onboarding checklist contains items and events that need to occur before, during, and after your new employee's first day, such as announcing their arrival to your current employees beforehand and completing basic human resources forms. Additional items may include providing your new employee with a facility tour, basic safety orientation training, and introducing them to their co-workers. I also suggest you, yourself, or their immediate supervisor, consider a practice to take each new employee out for lunch on their first day. Or you may consider providing lunch for your new and all current employees on your new employee's first day to create a more social opportunity for everyone to get to know each other. Depending on the position filled and your company structure, it may be a good idea and/or necessary that your new employee also visit your other business facilities, customers, and suppliers.

I propose a properly designed and executed onboarding procedure will address the immediate business and personal needs of your new and current employees, especially during their first few days and weeks. I also suggest your onboarding procedure will encourage your new and current employees to start their relationship(s) "on the right foot" and your business will benefit as a result.

For More Information and Advice

Please contact us at www.chargeupyourpeoplebook.com and/or www.gbicego.com if you would like more information and advice for your human resources challenges such as your organization chart, job descriptions, designing your team, your hiring process, interviewing style and process, onboarding checklist and/or any other challenges—we are here to help.

CHAPTER 6

HUMAN RESOURCES – PART II

Career Planning

Career planning, similar to your interview methods, can be used as a benefit to attract the very best people available to your business. Career planning may start for every employee before they commence contributing to your business by establishing their position within your organization chart and their related job description. As you consider and meet each candidate in your interview process, I suggest you are deciding if they can add short and long term value to your business while they are deciding if the position is aligned with their short and long term career plan objectives. At times, a potential/current employee will consider/continue working within your business in a role(s) that they and you mutually consider as a *stepping stone* to another role(s). I also suggest a new employee will rarely join your company fully trained for their initial job and then remain in that job for the remainder of their working career. These are some reasons why career planning is so important to your potential and current employees and your business successes.

Career planning should be considered one of your company's most critical human resources functions since it supports your employees who in turn support your business. I recommend every new employee develop a formal career plan as soon as they join your company to confirm discussions during their interviews and to prioritize their contributions to your business. I also recommend each of your employees and their supervisor jointly determine their career plan short and long term goals and implement related action plans in alignment with your business targets.

I suggest each employee's career plan start with an evaluation or assessment of their own values, personality, characteristics, likes, dislikes, skills, education, strengths, weaknesses, and current/past work experiences. This first step may be the most critical part of one's career plan since it sets the foundation or starting point from which they and you shape the remainder of their career path within your business. Your second step is to identify what eventual role(s) your employee wants to pursue in your company, i.e. the absolute ultimate position(s) they desire within your firm even if they may not be currently qualified for the position. I suggest this step is valuable to you as the employer because it provides you an opportunity to determine your employee's ambition and if they can be considered a potential candidate for any senior business leadership role(s) in the future. Your third step is to identify what other role(s) can be used as *stepping stones*, and what additional training and experience(s) are required to help your employee become qualified for their career plan ultimate role(s). Your fourth step is to develop a timeline to accomplish each *stepping stone role(s)* and to acquire any additional training and experience(s). And finally, your fifth and last step is to implement each career plan action item(s) and ensure regular follow-up at least as a part of every performance review to monitor progress. I also suggest a copy of an employee's career plan at least be given to them and another copy be placed in their personnel file for future reference.

Performance Reviews

Performance reviews can be another important strategy to develop and support your employees within their career plans and to meet your business needs. I suggest those business leaders who do not place much importance on performance reviews may also be the same ones wondering why their businesses are not achieving their objectives and/or how to improve their employee morale. You may find regular formal employee reviews are more prevalent in larger organizations versus smaller ones where fewer people typically "wear many hats" and may not "have time" for performance reviews. I suggest placing a low priority for regular employee performance reviews may be a mistake. I also suggest regular employee performance reviews are as important as regular business performance and other metrics reviews for your company's success. Employee performance reviews also provide an opportunity to acknowledge and encourage your employees' good work and contributions to your business, and to develop action plans to address any areas for improvement.

Performance reviews can be categorized as formal and informal. Your formal performance review process may be based upon a document that can be completed by only an employee's supervisor or both the employee and their supervisor. I recommend your formal employee performance review process require both employee and their supervisor complete the same performance review document to initiate discussions when they compare their answers to each question. Depending on the complexity of the employee performance form, each employee's performance may be reviewed during a single longer or a series of shorter meetings. To help facilitate effective discussions during these critical meetings, I advise you ensure your supervisors are trained to conduct formal employee performance reviews. Damaging an employee and supervisor relationship and their morale(s) may be the last thing you want to have occur during and/or as a result of any formal employee performance review.

Your formal employee performance review frequency reflects how important you consider this strategy for your business growth. Typically, a new employee may work during a probationary period lasting a few or several months during which time both you, your business, and your new employee can confirm each other's compatibility. I recommend that you/their supervisor meet with each new employee after their first day, every week during their first month, and every month until the end of their probationary period to monitor your new employee's performance. Many companies conduct formal employee performance reviews only once a year, if at all, and typically before any announcement of annual wage increases and/or bonuses. I recommend you consider completing at least one or two *major* performance reviews a year with semi-annual or quarterly updates in between each, i.e. a total of two or four reviews per year. I suggest you may find that semi-annual or quarterly updates may be an effective means to encourage continued progress and to adjust plans to achieve employees' goals before their one or two major annual review(s).

Informal employee performance reviews may be just as, if not perhaps more, significant than formal employee performance reviews. Informal employee performance reviews may occur when a supervisor stops to acknowledge an employee's contribution, or a job well done, or to coach an employee about an unacceptable action and/or behaviour. Informal employee performance reviews may typically occur more frequently than formal ones, and I recommend you and your business leaders practice a *managing by walking around* strategy. You may be told by an employee during their formal performance review that you already mentioned a certain issue(s) during a past conversation(s)—I suggest you consider this statement as evidence that you regularly and effectively completed your informal performance reviews.

Succession Planning

Succession planning, similar to career planning, can be a powerful and another important strategy to attract the best available people currently outside your business and to retain key current employees within your company. You may be surprised how some business leaders pay little or no attention to succession planning despite its significance for their company's day-to-day operations, long term survival, and to their employees' career plan objectives. Have you considered what may or may not happen to your business if you and/or one of your senior leaders could not physically be there and/or be involved for a significant period of time? These can be sobering questions that may keep you up at night unless you develop and maintain an effective succession plan to address such scenarios. I recommend you start developing a formal documented succession plan as soon as possible in case you do not currently have one.

Your succession planning process is interconnected with your employee career planning processes and training programs. I suggest your effective succession plan starts with identifying all the critical positions/functions within your company, at least with your own and that of all your senior business leaders' positions. You may expand your business succession planning to middle management and other employee positions after or simultaneously while planning for your own and senior leadership positions. Your second succession plan step is to identify and document all critical functions and competencies required for each position. Your third step is to identify potential candidates to fill each position who ideally are current employees; your career planning process can identify such employees. You may need to adjust an employee's career plan and training objectives to allow them to acquire the required skills and experience(s) to fill a critical position identified in your succession plan(s). If you may not have a current employee as a potential candidate for a critical position(s), I recommend you arrange for someone outside your business to temporarily fill that role(s) in the short term while you develop a current or new employee(s) to do so over the long term. The fourth and last succession planning step is to monitor each candidate's progress in their ability to fill their identified critical position(s).

I recommend you conduct *succession planning trial runs* versus waiting for an unplanned emergency to invoke your business succession plans. For example, you could plan to "disappear" for a few days/weeks on vacation and see what happens or doesn't happen during your absence. As stated in a previous chapter, I suggest this is your true leadership test. Upon your return, I suggest you review any issue(s) that arose during your absence, how well they were dealt with, and then adjust your succession plans accordingly. I also recommend you plan and conduct similar succession plan trials for all your critical company positions identified in your business succession plan.

I recall one personal experience when the business owner, also my supervisor, suddenly disappeared without notice for a few consecutive weeks after leaving the company on a Friday afternoon soon after he hired me as General Manager to replace him and assume responsibility for business operations. Even I, as the senior business leader in his absence, wasn't aware of his planned or unintended lengthy departure. Before this event, the business owner, for decades, was present at his company practically every day whenever he was in town and always announced any upcoming absences. So, you can imagine how some of my senior managers and employees were shocked during the following Monday and subsequent mornings when the business owner seemed to "disappear without a trace." My reply was that it was not relevant at the moment to know the current whereabouts of the business owner because we were all hired to contribute to the successful operation of the business within our positions even when the owner is not present. So I continued running the business with the help of my senior managers and our employees as usual. Of course, I made some inquiries about the business owner's whereabouts but received no information. During the owner's absence, our company was severely tested with several customer and internal challenges where we persevered in every case. After a few consecutive weeks of their absence, I was contacted by the owner who told me he was delighted and encouraged how I and my teams ran the business during his absence and now feels he can pursue other business objectives with his time. A few days later, in the morning, I happened to meet the owner in the kitchen; my first words were, "Oh, you must be new here; let me introduce myself." We both laughed and went about our work.

I advise you consider succession planning as one of your most important tasks as a business leader and that it should be a regular priority in your thinking. Without much *bench strength* on your business team, I suggest you may be the only other person to complete vital business tasks, thus limiting your business growth and own personal freedom. Effective succession planning may also help prevent any power struggles between your key employees due to your own or another critical person's absence that may damage your business operations. Successful succession planning will provide your key employees an attractive career path that will encourage them to remain and grow within your business. And, finally, you may find it necessary to create another business division(s) that also contributes to increased sales and profits, to satisfy some of your key employees' career plan objectives linked to your succession plan—this is great news in my opinion.

Training

Training, similar to succession and career planning, can be another important and effective strategy to attract the best available people currently outside your company and to retain key current employees within your business. Similar to succession and career planning, I recommend employee training can start before and/or on your new employee's first day as part of their onboarding or orientation process. I also recommend you establish and regularly review each employee's training requirements as part of their career planning, performance reviews, and succession planning objectives. Similar to other critical areas of your business operations, I suggest you create and review an annual training strategic plan to identify your training goals, methods, budgets, and timelines to coordinate all your training initiatives.

An overall training and skills matrix is useful to summarize requirements for each company position, and to identify any gaps for each employee in their current and future position(s) identified in their career plan. The first step to creating your overall training and skills matrix is to list your company positions in columns across the top of the page; you may find it useful to group positions within their own departments. Your second step is to list your training and skill requirements/programs in rows on the left side of the page; similarly, you may find it beneficial to group them into categories such as safety, quality, computer software, leadership, communications, and other job specific categories. Your third step will be to identify which trainings and skills are required for each company position. You may find some training and skills requirements may be common to all positions such as general safety training, whereas most others may be specific to certain groups of positions. Your fourth step is to determine the current status of each employee's trainings and skills for their current position(s). These reviews now place you and your employees in a position to begin planning any additional trainings and skills required for their current position(s) and future position(s) identified in their career and succession plans. The sum of your individual employee training schedules can then be used to develop your overall training budget for the upcoming month, quarter, and fiscal year.

Depending on the size of your company, its structure, and number of employees, you may consider employing a training coordinator who may also assume other administrative duties. Your training coordinator can develop your annual training strategic plan, budget, and any other documents such as a training request form. The training coordinator will also process all completed and approved training request forms, maintain your overall training and skills matrix, and update each employee's individual training plan. They can also schedule all training sessions and remind employees and their supervisors beforehand to adjust their schedules accordingly. Your training coordinator can also prepare internal training rooms, ensure the availability of supplies, food and drinks, make any travel and accommodations arrangements for external training sessions, and process all training certificates.

I also recommend every employee receive a training certificate for every training course they complete, regardless if they were trained internally or outside your company. I suggest you do not distribute training certificates to any employee as soon as they've completed each training but instead consider presenting them to your employees at regularly scheduled employee communications meetings. This practice may enhance your employees' experiences of receiving their training certificates, provide an opportunity to be acknowledged by more people for their achievements, and demonstrates the significance you place on training. I also recommend you make two copies and frame each training certificate—one copy to be presented to each employee and a second copy hung on any and every common wall in your facility. Imagine the impression it will make on your employees and reinforce the importance you place on training when all your common area walls are filled top to bottom with training certificates.

I also advise you consider implementing a policy to reimburse employees for training courses that are or may not be job-related. You can consider establishing certain reimbursement guidelines such as paying for tuition upon receiving proof your employee(s) successfully completed their training, whereas your employee(s) is responsible to pay for their books and other course materials. Or you may consider budgeting some monies to pay all expenses for any non-job related course(s) your employees may want to pursue as long as they provide evidence of their completion.

Employee Information, Files & Records

The most important advice I can offer about your employees' personal and employment associated information is to ensure your company always treats such data as private and confidential and with maximum discretion at all times. I suggest your business has an obligation to ensure all your employees' personal and employment related information is always protected, and access to such data remains limited to as few people as necessary. I suggest tolerating lax storage and maintenance of your employees' personal and work related information may result in legal issues for your business and/or lack of trust from your employees. The best way to protect your employees' personal and work related information (at least in paper form) is to store any documents within locked filing cabinets. I suggest you locate those filing cabinets containing employee personnel files within a limited access area with a key or keyless lock door.

Another strategy to enhance the protection your employees' personnel information is to store their files and associated documents in one single location. Some businesses may find it convenient to store basic employee personnel information in their front office, safety training records in the safety office, quality and other training records in the quality office, and any discipline letters in various supervisor offices. I caution this *dispersed method* of employee personnel information storage increases the chances of such information "ending up in the wrong hands." I recommend all your employee personnel documents be stored in a single secured location and that any copies be destroyed immediately. You may also find it more convenient to separate your employee files into categories such hourly or salary paid, or by department, and then limit access to each group(s) of employee personnel files accordingly.

On occasion, you may be faced with an employee's argument that they have the right to access their employee file and remove or at least make copies of any document(s) within their employee personnel file at any time. My advice is to first consult your employment law lawyer on such matters. In my opinion, your employee personnel files and their associated documents are solely the property of your company and your employees may not have the legal right to examine, remove, or copy any information. Your company may of course, in good faith, consider allowing such employee examinations of their specific personnel file on a case by case basis. Once again, I recommend you consult your employment law lawyer to address any questions or concerns about this and any other related employment issue.

As a final piece of advice regarding employee information, I suggest you have a policy that all employees are responsible to update your human resources department with any changes to their personal information such as emergency contacts, addresses, phone numbers, marital status, and new family members. As a backup plan, you may find it useful to confirm each employee's basic contact information every one or two years.

Employee Compensation

Employee compensation has always been and may always be a topic of passionate debates. One reason for this fact is that many people believe there is typically only one practical reason many/most of your employees come to work: money or pay in the form of hourly wages, salaries, and bonuses. I suggest there may be other reasons as well: health benefits for themselves and families, to be personally challenged, to be social and have human interaction, and/or a sincere desire to help your business solve an issue(s) and/or challenge(s). Considering these reasons explaining why your employees show up to work every day, how much should you pay your employees, i.e. just "enough," average, or above average wages?

I recommend you consider compensating your employees as much as you can and offer them as many benefits as possible within the constraints of your business finances. This compensation philosophy may sound different; in fact, it perhaps may sound completely opposite to other employers' policies, and may be at the moment impractical for your business. But I recommend you, as have I, consider implementing this thinking for two reasons: 1. you may attract better quality people who tend to be self-starters (thus helping free up more of your time to focus on other more value-added activities), and 2. it helps retain your employees over the years (thus allowing them to continue growing and contributing within your business and helps avoid expensive turnover costs). I suggest you consider from a pragmatic point of view, what a five to perhaps twenty percent employee compensation over-payment may really cost your business compared to the sometimes up to fifty to one hundred-plus percent additional benefits that may be realized by your business as a result of hiring and paying the best most talented people. Again, I suggest you consider implementing this philosophy as much it makes sense for your business. If you think this philosophy may not be practical in any business, I suggest you research employee compensation packages of the top-ranked and most successful businesses in the world. Although some employee compensation packages may seem unconventional, I suggest top-ranked and most successful companies continue to offer them because they are effective to attract and retain the best people available.

Your total compensation plan may be comprised of several components such as take-home pay (either salary, hourly, and/or partly based on commissions) and various benefits such as health and dental cost coverage (typically at least partially paid by you as the employer). You may consider several compensation plan enhancements to attract and retain the best employees possible such as paying the full cost of health and dental benefits, allowing brand name drugs in addition to or instead of generic drugs, and extending such benefits to all employees, i.e. both full-time and part-time, and/or both salary-paid and hourly-paid employees. Additional compensation plan enhancements may include increased benefit plan limits for all health and dental services, and increased plan scope benefits to include other health services. Retirement plans and company contributions that match or double your employees' contributions are very popular benefits. You may also consider adding an additional contribution to your employee's retirement plan if they decide to invest their entire annual bonus or profit sharing dividend into their retirement plan(s). And finally, you may consider offering an employee stock purchase plan to those employees who meet certain requirements.

If some of the above compensation plan items may not be currently feasible for your business (or even if they are), I recommend you consider implementing other *at work* benefits such as summer picnics for employees and their families, and an on-site or off-site holiday party for both employees and their partners and perhaps a separate party for their children. You may find that a weekly or bi-monthly barbeque lunch/dinner and/or family passes to nearby amusement parks may be other popular benefits appreciated by your employees. I suggest you consider employee sales and discounts for your company product and/or service if feasible, and celebrating everyone's birthday in a particular month by bringing in a catered lunch and/or birthday cake. You may also consider paying hourly-paid employees for the entire time they spend at work (i.e. also paying them during their lunches and breaks), and enforcing salary-paid employees to work only eight hours a day if their pay is based on forty hours per week (i.e. five days times eight hours per day). In addition to these *at work* benefits, there are additional *time away from work* benefits.

Time away from work benefits may include permitting both full-time and part-time, and both salaried-paid and hourly-paid employees, to be paid for any sick days, to leave early on Fridays either during summer months or year-round, or to take every Friday off but work longer hours from Monday to Thursday. Of course, I recommend you investigate how such policies may affect your business operations, customers, and suppliers before implementing them. You may even have heard that some employers are experimenting with the policy of infinite vacations for all employees (i.e. take as much vacation time as you'd like, provided of course your work is done and/or your position duties will be covered by others during your time away). Other *time away from work* benefits may include offering longer vacation times for all employees, paid leave of absences, and allowing employees to carry over any vacation time from year to year or be reimbursed for any remaining vacation time at the end of a vacation year. Still more *time away from work* benefits may include fully paid days off for jury duty, bereavement, or the birth of a new child.

Additional benefits, part of executive compensation packages, may include car allowances, auto insurance, fuel, repairs and maintenance costs paid by the company, company vehicles, and sometimes the use of company jets. Other executive benefits may include flying business and/or first class on commercial flights or by private jet, sometimes staying at certain hotel chains, and meal and clothing allowances. You and your business may also consider offering interest-free loans, gym memberships, golf and country club memberships, chauffeur and limousine services, residences paid for by the company, and stock options. I caution though that such *executive* benefits and perks have come under increasing scrutiny in both public and private companies over time; therefore, I recommend you exercise discretion and prudence if you are considering to offer them. In fact, I suggest you consider reducing and/or eliminating some or most of these perks if that makes sense for your business.

Sales commission bonuses are in a different category than most other types of compensation. Some business leaders may think compensation based partly or solely on commissions is the only *true* measure of the value an individual contributes to a business and/or marketplace; in many ways, you may agree with this statement as do I. A sales commission plan, if feasible for some or all your employees, may be the most fair and equitable form of compensation since its rewards are typically related to an individual's and/or a group's efforts and skills. But there may be some sales commissions plan realities that may cause this system to be *less than fair*, such a person or group being awarded a more *customer-rich* territory and/or market, or being based on how much a person or group can sell above budget. These sales commissions' compensation plan realities may even have adverse effects on the rest of your business. Let me explain with a personal experience.

Every year, our company completed a business plan and budget exercise starting with a sales budget on which the remaining departments developed their respective plans and budgets. Although we hired temporary employees every year due to seasonal product demands, it seemed we always needed to hire more temporary employees than was budgeted a few short months ago. I never quite understood the cause(s) behind our *over budget* temporary employee annual hiring until I was promoted to the vice president operations position and began attending monthly corporate meetings. During my investigations, I discovered our sales peoples' compensation plan bonuses were based upon how much they sold over their own individual sales budgets set earlier in the year. I suspected each salesperson tried to *low ball* their individual annual sales budget and then worked to *over achieve* them to maximize their bonuses. I recall being told the sales compensation plan in its current form "has always been this way" and besides, higher sales were a benefit for everyone in the company because it offered more work and higher profits as well. I replied that higher sales may be beneficial for some people except me who needed to explain to our new corporate leadership team why I am *over budget* with my labour costs at times. So, I prepared my defence showing how our past actual sales dollars surpassed our budgeted sales dollars, how our sales peoples' individual compensation plan bonuses were based on how much they *over sold* their artificially low budget sales budgets while our actual labour costs were lower this versus last year as a percentage of sales (although my current year labour cost dollars were *over budget*). Let's say my presentation and defense caused some "interesting" conversations and subsequent changes to next year's sales compensation plan. The new corporate leadership also thanked me for presenting these facts and complimented me on how well I ran our business operations.

I recommend you design your compensation plan(s) after determining your business goals and what preferred behaviours you expect from your employees, similar to designing your job descriptions during or after developing your organization chart. You can consider several factors to determine each of your employees' individual compensation, and their individual annual bonuses, such as their individual performance to achieve their annual work goals, their seniority and position, any culpable absenteeism and/or tardiness. I also recommend you consider rewarding each of your employees as part of a group compensation plan focused on achieving overall business targets.

Group compensation methods such as profit sharing may be effective to achieve your overall business goals by requiring all your employees to collectively strive to achieve them. In reality, group compensation strategies may encourage your employees to regulate themselves whenever they see waste or any other action(s) by their fellow co-workers that may affect business profits and thus their annual group bonus. Your group profit sharing plan may be based upon achieving various business operations targets for safety, quality, productivity, and overall company profits. You may also assign a *weight* or contribution factor for each profit sharing plan item while each profit sharing plan item's score is based on the difference between the year's final result and its target typically set at the beginning of the fiscal year during your budget process. Similar to a decision matrix, your overall group profit sharing plan factor may be calculated by summing up the multiplication of each profit sharing plan item contribution factor times their score. You may also include other individual employee items such as their position and seniority to determine each employee's final group profit sharing plan factor. Then, each individual employee's annual bonus is calculated as their final profit sharing plan factor times their current or past years' annual base salary, or total hourly earnings, including or not including overtime pay.

Depending on your corporate culture, you may decide to base part or all of your employee compensation on individual and/or group efforts. I recommend you consider that a combination of both individual and group bonus compensation, based on overall company performance, may be the most effective strategy to motivate your employees to achieve their personal and your business goals. By implementing a mix of individual and group bonus compensation, your employees may receive an enhanced bonus if both they, individually, and your company perform well that year, or at least some bonus based on their individual contributions, even if your business may not have performed well financially that year. Naturally, I suggest all employee compensation should be awarded based on your company's financial performance.

I suggest the variety of employee benefits is only limited by your own imagination, and the imagination of your employees. I also suggest you develop and implement a compensation system that supports all your business values and goals. I recommend you review and modify your compensation plan on a periodic basis to reflect any major changes in your business and/or market places. And, as I have stated several times throughout this book, I always recommend that, as the business leader, you should base your decisions on whatever makes sense for your business.

Payroll

I recommend your business payroll activities be administered by a detail oriented and experienced individual(s), preferably formally educated in accounting and very knowledgeable about your business jurisdiction employment standards in addition to your company payroll policies and practices. Since the person(s) responsible for your payroll activities provides a critical service to your employees and business, I advise you ensure this person(s) is responsible, dependable and dedicated to ensure everyone gets paid accurately and on time, every pay period, no matter what. I also advise you ensure your payroll person(s) has an alternate person(s) who will complete these critical duties on occasion when they may be absent from work for whatever reason(s). You may also find it advantageous to divide your payroll activities between two people, one for hourly-paid and the other for salary-paid employees. I also recommend you process your payroll activities using a computer-based payroll system which may also be used by your payroll person(s) to track, or at least have access to (perhaps also design and implement), your employee vacation and time and attendance systems.

You may be old enough to remember when time and attendance systems consisted of employees who "punched a clock" upon arriving and leaving their workplace. Sometimes employees' attendance was, and still is, currently monitored by their supervisor at the start of their work shift as was/is done in elementary and/or high schools. Technology advances have led to the use of swipe cards and biometric measures such as hand, fingerprint, and eye scans to collect employee time and attendance information. Whatever your employee time and attendance data collection method(s), I recommend the immediate supervisor of each employee regularly review and adjust, if necessary, all time and attendance data issues before submitting this data to your payroll department. I also recommend you require your supervisor(s)/manager(s) to regularly justify (and you review) any overtime hours and costs. Overtime costs may be required to meet increased customer demands at times, but may also be a sign of production issues and/or perhaps mismanagement of business resources.

The manner in which employee pay has been distributed has also changed with time. Again, you may be old enough or aware of the practice of being paid every week with cash (dollar bills and some change) in a small envelope, or by cheque that was required to be personally deposited at a bank—there are some employers who still use these methods to pay their employees. With the Internet and electronic money transactions, employee wages may now be paid via direct deposit to each employee's individual bank account. If your company has not already done so, I recommend you implement a direct-deposit payroll system to take advantage of its enhanced security and convenience for both your business and your employees. Direct deposit payroll receipts can also be issued to employees at the same time as their pay direct deposits are electronically completed. You may consider mailing direct deposit receipts to your employees' home addresses, although I advise against this practice since the direct deposit payroll receipt may not arrive at all, be tampered by others, or cause unintended consequences within their home.

I recommend you never delegate the task of distributing payroll receipts to *just anyone*. To the contrary, I suggest the act of delivering payroll receipts, paycheques, and payroll payments can be a very useful and powerful occurrence that enhances and confirms the authority of and respect for the person delivering them, even though direct deposit payroll receipts and/or pay cheques are not real money. I discourage you from permitting anyone else except your employees' direct supervisor(s)/manager(s) to distribute payroll direct deposit receipts, paycheques, or payroll payments, since they may not appreciate their importance to your employees. You may also consider having the same supervisor(s)/manager(s) distribute any other payments such as business expenses, cheques, and/or annual bonus cheques, or you may want to reserve those duties for yourself or your designate(s).

What should you do if there is no money available for any employee pay and/or benefit increases? My advice is to inform your employees before any expectations "get out of hand" and then explain the reason(s) and/or cause(s) for the lack of employee pay increases and/or benefits reductions. This may be a tough discussion filled with emotions and frustrations, but I suggest the vast majority of your employees will appreciate your honesty and candor. Trust me, your employees are not stupid—they may or will realize, even before you formally announce a pay freeze and/or benefits reduction, that the business is experiencing some difficulties.

What should you do if you have only some or a little money available for pay increases that may not "be enough" for everyone? I suggest you consider doing what I did at one time when faced with this dilemma: I first allocated some money and increased some individuals' pay whose current compensation was relatively too low (as I do every year), froze all the compensation of all salaried-paid employees, and evenly distributed the remaining monies among all my hourly-paid employees. Yes, I received complaints from some of my salary-paid employees (no increase) and also from some of my hourly paid employees (not enough increase), but this strategy was the best and most fair one I could think of at that time. Being a business leader may be challenging, especially during financially difficult times— hopefully you and your employees will work together to ensure better pay increases and/or benefits in the future.

My final piece of advice regarding payroll: when a reasonable payroll mistake occurs, I recommend you fix it immediately, confirm the accuracy and cause(s) of that mistake, and then implement corrective actions to prevent any recurrence. Sometimes payroll errors occur and at times an upset employee requests and needs an immediate restitution. My advice is to reimburse the affected employee what they think they are owed as soon as possible for two reasons: 1. who knows what each employee deserves to be paid for that pay period better than they do, them or your payroll person(s) who administers your entire payroll?, and 2. this action demonstrates you trust and support your employee. On the other hand, I recommend you take immediate and appropriate action(s) against any employee when you confirm evidence of fraud may have been committed when correcting a false payroll "mistake."

For More Information and Advice

Please contact us at www.chargeupyourpeoplebook.com and/or www.gbicego.com if you would like more information and advice for your human resources challenges such as career planning, performance reviews, succession planning, training, employee information, files and records, employee compensation, payroll and/or any other challenges—we are here to help.

CHAPTER 7

HUMAN RESOURCES – PART III

Employee Handbook & Policies

I recommend your business, even if you employ one other person besides yourself, have an employee handbook documenting your company human resources policies, practices, and guidelines. Your employee handbook should include a statement about your commitment to supporting and working with all your employees in a fair and respectful manner, and how all employees should work in a similar manner with each other. I suggest you also include statements and/or sections about your company's commitment to health and safety, the environment, workplace harassment, and workplace violence. Your employee handbook should also include company policies, practices, and guidelines such as how new employees are hired, when employees permanently leave under different circumstances, and how and when employees may temporarily leave for vacations, sick days, jury duty, and other reasons. Your employee handbook should also include basic information about employee compensation and benefits, hours of work, confidential information, intellectual property, and where employees can park their vehicles during their working hours. I also suggest your employee handbook outline requirements and/or expectations from management and all employees in situations such as with whom and when any employee should raise an issue(s) of concern. As well, your employee handbook should outline a broad set of general rules of behaviour from no horseplay to accepting any gifts from suppliers. Disciplinary procedures should also be explained in detail that company management will follow in the event that an employee violates any practice, guideline, or policy.

Similar to many of your business documents, your employee handbook, its policies, practices, and guidelines may be subject to changes and improvements as applicable laws are introduced/ amended and additional issues present themselves within your business. I recommend you document within your employee handbook that its policies, practices, and guidelines are subject to change at any time. I also advise all your employee handbook policy changes be formally announced in employee meetings, memos, and emails to ensure that such change(s) are implemented effectively and without issue(s). You may also consider a suitable notice period before implementing a new and/or revised policy, especially if it may significantly affect current employees.

I suggest you conduct training sessions to introduce all your current employees to the policies, practices, and guidelines contained within it, especially if you are writing and implementing your company's first employee handbook. And, as part of every new employee orientation process, I also advise your new employee be given a brief but detailed employee handbook review; this briefing may require as much as an hour or more.

As my final piece of advice regarding employee handbooks, I recommend your employment law lawyer(s) review your employee handbook before you publish and implement it. I also advise every employee sign an acknowledge form (may be the last and a perforated page of your employee handbook) which should be subsequently placed in their respective employee file(s). The employee handbook acknowledgement form should state that the employee has been trained, informed, had an opportunity(ies) to ask questions about the handbook and its contents, and that the employee handbook's policies, practices, and guidelines form a part of their employment contract with your business.

Disciplinary Policies & Practices

Some business leaders and managers may be intimidated by and/or hesitant to apply their own disciplinary process resulting in no employee disciplinary actions as required, whereas others practically ignore their disciplinary policies when disciplining employees and whose disciplinary actions may be excessive. I suggest both these extremes of inactions and actions may place your business operations and company in peril. I recommend it is crucial that every disciplinary action is reasonable, fair, and the consequences of any policy violation is proportional with each inappropriate employee behaviour and/or action. I also suggest you always consider any past similar or other incident(s) associated with any particular employee in question and other employees' similar unacceptable action(s) and/or behaviour(s) when deciding a particular employee's disciplinary action(s). Done correctly, your company's disciplinary actions will effectively modify and address any employee's unacceptable behaviours and actions and not *target* them as a person. Done incorrectly, your company's disciplinary actions may damage your employee morale, have other unintended consequences for your business and its operations, and result in litigation, expensive legal bills, and other damages. I strongly recommend you consider consulting your employment law lawyer if you have any concerns/questions before implementing any employee disciplinary action(s).

It is crucial that your disciplinary policy and procedures are clearly outlined in your employee handbook. I advise you consider using a multiple step disciplinary procedure, including termination of employment as the last discipline step, to address any unacceptable employee action and/or behaviour. Each subsequent discipline level is considered more severe or *serious* than the previous one. My advice is to also state in every formal written disciplinary letter that continued unacceptable action(s) and/or behaviour(s) will result in further disciplinary action(s), including termination of employment, even in an employee's first level discipline letter. I suggest this strategy removes the potential argument that the employee was not aware of the ultimate result of their continued or repeated unacceptable action(s) and/or behaviour(s). Perhaps you may also consider stating your discipline procedure steps or levels documented in your employee handbook within every employee discipline letter as well.

You may be considering at times if you should issue a first level discipline letter for one unacceptable behaviour, a second level letter for another different unacceptable behaviour, and a third level letter for another different unacceptable behaviour, etc. to "fast track" or expedite an employee's departure from your company. I caution you may be *targeting* an employee if you may be thinking about this strategy. As with many employment law issues, I recommend you consult your employment law lawyer before proceeding with this course of action. It is clear that you, as an employer, have the right and may do whatever you think is appropriate when implementing your discipline policy and handling your business affairs, but, of course, all actions have consequences.

I recommend it is more prudent to issue subsequent *levels* of discipline for each specific or unique unacceptable action(s) and/or behaviour(s) to better defend against any "targeting" accusation(s) when disciplining any employee. For example, you may issue a first-level discipline to an employee the first time they come to work late, then another first-level discipline if that same employee is caught smoking for the first time in the workplace, and so on. Any subsequent recurrence of an unacceptable action(s) and/or behaviour(s) committed by the same employee will result in the next level disciplinary action(s) for that unacceptable action(s) and/or behaviour(s). This may result in a situation where an employee may currently have only one discipline letter for coming to work late, and perhaps three letters for smoking in the workplace while still being employed by your company. Although my advice may seem as giving some employees too many chances, I propose that any employee who constantly violates your employee handbook policies and guidelines will eventually give you sufficient reasons to terminate their employment. And when you do terminate such a person's employment, I suggest your actions will better protect you and your business from any potential legal action(s) and fraudulent "targeting" accusations. I also recommend you consult your employment law lawyer before terminating anyone's employment.

I cannot stress enough the importance that you must always ensure your formal written disciplinary process and actions are never used or perceived to be used (although you may be unfairly accused of it) as a personal vendetta/attack or to "target" any employee. I suggest the last thing you want for your business is to be proven guilty of favouritism where you avoid disciplining an employee(s) for an unacceptable action and/or behaviour when warranted, while exclusively disciplining another employee(s) for that same/similar unacceptable action and/or behaviour. Do not be surprised, though, if you and your other business leaders may be accused of favouritism and/or "targeting" anyway, since some people may make such false accusations to avoid receiving any justified disciplinary action(s) themselves. If deemed necessary, I recommend you immediately reverse any disciplinary action(s) that are proven to be the result of "targeting" other employees and discipline those other leaders/supervisors who unfairly issued such disciplinary action(s).

I also recommend you always remain focused on your employees' unacceptable action(s) and/or behaviour(s), and not on what they may have said when considering to implement any disciplinary action(s), i.e. remain focused on your employee's actions and behaviours and not on their words. Some people may make statements and use words during a confrontation that are clearly inappropriate, especially if done so *in the heat of the moment*. Your frustration with an employee's statements and/or words may be understandable; perhaps you feel you did not deserve such a comment(s), or you conclude and/or know their statement(s) may be false. I suggest that you, as a business leader, should effectively disseminate between statements and words made "in the heat of the moment" and real threats, exercise prudence, judgement, rise above any petty comments, and ensure all formal disciplinary actions are fair and consistent across all levels of your company.

A clear exception to this above recommendation is when any employee and/or other person threatens or commits any action(s) of discrimination, harassment and/or violence—then I recommend you immediately implement your workplace harassment and/or violence procedures. Especially if any employee has made any threat of violence, I strongly advise you require that employee to leave the premises immediately, not only for the safety of the remaining employees but also for their own personal safety. I suggest you may need to offer to pay the offending employee for the remainder of their work shift to entice them to leave voluntarily. I also advise you may need to contact the police to remove an aggressive employee so you may conduct your investigation afterwards.

The timing of your disciplinary action(s) may also be critical to ensure its justification and effectiveness to address an employee's unacceptable actions(s) and/or behaviour(s) and to safeguard your own credibility. I recommend you investigate any unacceptable employee action and/or behaviour as quickly as possible, and that any suitable disciplinary action(s) be issued immediately thereafter. You may also be wondering how much time needs to, or should, pass until you issue an additional disciplinary action to the same employee who is repeating the same unacceptable action(s) and/or behaviour(s). On one hand, you may consider disciplining your employee as often and quickly as possible until *they get the message*. On the other hand, I suggest you may want to be careful to avoid terminating their employment at the same time unless warranted. I recommend you consider restarting an employee at their first discipline level if they have no documented disciplinary actions within the last twenty-four months, unless there was some very *major* unacceptable action(s) and/or behaviour(s) in the past. Once again, I advise you consult your employment law lawyer on these matters and you, as the employer, have the right to discipline your employees as you see fit but, of course, your actions are always subject to potential consequences.

I recommend you may consider executing any formal disciplinary action(s) as a last resort when addressing an employee's inappropriate behaviour and/or action. On occasion, an informal and sincere verbal reminder may be a more effective strategy and a better investment of your time and efforts when addressing an employee's unacceptable action(s) and/or behaviour(s)—some people may just need to be reminded at times. You may document these verbal reminders as "coaching" and place your notes about any coaching conversations or sessions into the employee's personnel file.

I also recommend that you and all your business leaders document every employee "coaching" conversation, event(s), and observation(s) that may be reasonably useful in future potential disciplinary actions. This discipline may seem challenging because your workday(s) may be filled with numerous priorities and it may seem easier at that moment to just postpone this simple task requiring a few minutes of your time. You may be relieved you recorded some important and relevant conversation points and/or observation(s) at the time of an event instead of trying to recall details at a later time when it may not be appropriate to proceed with disciplinary actions because you may have forgotten some key details. Without accurate notes about an incident that should be recorded as soon as possible, I suggest you may not rely exclusively upon your memory of an incident to help you make better decisions about possibly disciplining an employee in the future.

Depending on each set of circumstances, you may have reached the point where you need to consider implementing your disciplinary procedures after an employee commits an unacceptable action(s) and/or behaviour(s), regardless if you have had no, or some, coaching conversations with that employee. Don't be surprised if an employee may initially express their disagreement to receiving any disciplinary action(s) as a consequence(s) of their unacceptable action(s) and/or behaviour(s)—this is normal in my opinion. At this point, I suggest you effectively turn the discussion back to them by telling your employee it is their unacceptable action(s) and/or their behaviour(s) that will determine the consequences of such actions and/or behaviours; I suggest you state you are just *doing your job*. I also recommend you clarify, in a non-threatening tone, they will avoid any further disciplinary action(s) if and when they stop their unacceptable action(s) and/or behaviour(s). Hopefully, your employee will get the message that their fate will be determined by their actions and/or behaviours, and not by you personally. If your employee continues with their unacceptable action(s) and/or behaviour(s), I suggest you have no other practical choice but to proceed implementing additional appropriate disciplinary action(s).

A witness(es) can be a critical factor in any disciplinary procedure, especially if there may be an unacceptable action and/or behaviour that occurred during a conversation between two people. Without a witness, I propose it is more challenging to enforce any disciplinary action(s) to address any issue(s) associated with a conversation between two people. Without a witness(es) to an inappropriate conversation, you may be left with a "they said/they said" and/or "they did/they did" argument which may be practically impossible to resolve fairly. My advice is to proceed with disciplinary action(s) to address any unacceptable actions(s)/behaviour(s) between two people in a conversation only if you have a witness to that conversation, unless there are extenuating circumstances otherwise. If there isn't a witness, it may be more effective to coach and/or warn both parties that any future repeated unacceptable action(s)/

behaviour(s) during a conversation may be dealt with in a different manner.

Implementing Disciplinary Actions

So, you've investigated an incident and decided that a disciplinary letter is warranted to document your employee's unacceptable action(s) and/or behaviour(s). To begin with, I recommend every formal discipline letter be printed on your company letterhead to emphasize its importance and communicate the seriousness of the issue with your employee(s). I also advise each discipline letter's length be one page if possible, dated when the discipline is issued (not when the letter was designed), addressed to the employee with their correct residential address, and also denote the manner in which the letter was delivered to the employee. I also recommend to include the term "Private and Confidential," centered on the very top line, followed by the title, "Discipline Letter," on the second line, and a subject line describing the discipline level. Each discipline letter should begin by stating the date, time, and location of the infraction, briefly describing the unacceptable action(s) and/or behaviour(s) and any witness(es). Subsequently list the date and subject of any past disciplinary letters after which you request your employee to correct their unacceptable action(s) and/or behaviour(s) immediately or within a reasonable time limit. I also advise you offer your employee assistance to correct their unacceptable action(s) and/or behaviour(s) after which you restate your disciplinary policy levels up to and including termination of their employment. Then, leave space for the signatures and dates of the letter issuer, your witness, and the employee. I also recommend you reference that two copies of the discipline letter have been made; one will be distributed to the employee and the other to the employee's personnel file. Finally, I advise each disciplinary letter be reviewed at least by your human resources department and/or your employment law lawyer as appropriate before its delivery to your employee.

I also recommend a witness be present at every discipline meeting, preferably who is not directly associated with the employee being disciplined, as a precaution to counter any unsubstantiated accusations and to observe the meeting proceedings. As an additional benefit, the presence of a witness during a disciplinary action meeting may also dissuade either party from committing any unacceptable action(s) and/or behaviour(s). As I've already stated, without a witness you may be left with a "they said/they said" or "they did/they did" situation that may be practically impossible to resolve. I suggest a witness' responsibilities should be limited to observation, remaining silent no matter what is said and/or happens during the meeting, and signing the discipline letter—any other action(s) may be construed as inappropriate.

With the two discipline letter copies in hand (signed only by you at this point) and witness ready, it's now time to complete the discipline meeting. I suggest your employee be called to an office by a manager/supervisor where the discipline issuer and witness will be waiting for them. Once the employee enters the room, close the door behind them and briefly explain the purpose of the discipline meeting and letter, and the subsequent disciplinary action(s) resulting from their unacceptable action(s) and/or behaviour(s). I cannot emphasize enough the importance that your statements be brief and to the point, and your tone of voice, posture and other non-verbal communication be non-threatening, and to at least keep your emotions *in check*. Your employee may become emotional and/or upset to which I advise you reply that this action is "nothing personal" nor directed against them as a person. I suggest you continue emphasizing that you are addressing the person's unacceptable action(s) and/or behaviour(s) and not them as a person, and that the disciplinary meeting and action is the consequence of their unacceptable action(s) and/or behaviour(s). Also remind your employee they can avoid any further disciplinary action(s) if and when they cease their unacceptable action(s) and/or behaviour(s). I also suggest you avoid *getting sucked in* or *taking the bait* of what may seem to be any unsubstantiated accusations.

As soon as you've stated what you needed to say, have the witness sign both copies of the discipline letter and ask the employee to do so as well. You may be wondering what can be done if the employee does not sign their discipline letter, and/or if the letter is still legal or useful without an employee's signature. This is when a witness' presence is vital. It has been my experience and is my opinion that any discipline letter not signed or agreed to by an employee is still valid; I strongly recommend you consult your employment law lawyer if you have any questions and/or concerns about this and/or any other employment law matter. Soon after the letter signing, deliver one copy of the discipline letter to the employee and conclude the meeting. In some cases, your employee may need some time to "collect themselves" before returning to work or may ask to leave for the rest of the day. I suggest you plan to temporarily replace your employee for the remainder of their work day if you conduct your disciplinary meeting earlier in their work shift. A well-executed discipline meeting duration should last no more than two to three minutes. I also recommend you make notes about the discipline meeting itself, detailing its time and place, the presence of the witness, and any other relevant information.

You may be wondering what you should or can do if the offending employee refuses to meet with you for a disciplinary action meeting. I suggest you address this possibility as I have done so in the past: approach the employee (in a non-threatening manner) at their work station with a witness and offer them two options: 1. execute the discipline letter right then and there, or 2. do so in private. Faced with this decision, most people will choose the private meeting option although you may need to rarely execute a discipline letter to an employee at their workstation. In a situation where an employee leaves work before a discipline letter is issued, I suggest you wait until they return to work or send the discipline letter to their home/mailing address via registered mail while keeping a proof of delivery with the discipline letter in their employee personnel file.

Termination and Layoff Procedures

Any decision to terminate anyone's employment should never be considered lightly. Although your termination decision may be deemed justified and necessary for your company and/or your remaining employee(s), I advise you remain mindful that all your business decisions affect peoples' lives and perhaps their family's lives too. I also recommend that you, as have I, base your termination and/or lay off decisions on the viewpoint that one or a few people may not be more important than the entire business itself and your remaining employees. You may find terminating someone's employment a bit nerve wracking—that's normal in my opinion. Personally, by the time I terminate anyone's employment for just cause and/or layoff anyone, I have assured myself that I have done everything possible to avoid such an event and/or that employee's employment termination and/or layoff was justified by their preceding action(s) and/or behaviour(s) and/or general business conditions. You may also feel, as I have, at times remorseful for the affected employee's family especially if you are terminating an employee for just cause—that's also normal in my opinion. In this case, I suggest you consider the perspective that if your employee valued their responsibility to support their family, they may or should not have committed unacceptable action(s) and/or behavior(s) that led to their employment termination. An exception to this point of view may be when an employee(s) must be laid off or terminated due to no fault of their own such as for general business and/or economic reasons.

My advice is to always treat people with respect in every situation, especially when you need to terminate someone's employment, temporarily or permanently layoff an employee(s), or if an employee(s) resigns. People may always remember how you treated them, especially when you have to let them go. Being temporarily or permanently laid off, or having your employment terminated, typically may be a very emotional life event. Your affected employee(s) may suddenly need to figure out how to sustain themselves and their families, and what to do with themselves over the next day(s), week(s) and month(s). I recommend you help your affected employees through this life transition process as much as you can while remaining compassionate, empathetic, fair, but firm. I also recommend you, being the person responsible to decide and/or implement layoffs and terminations, should also be mindful of your own emotional and physical health before, during, and after these events.

When is the best day and time of day to lay off an employee(s) or terminate their employment? I recommend you consider avoiding terminating anyone's employment or laying off anyone on a Monday because the event may be more shocking and adversely affect your employee who may become more grumpy, angry, or depressed than usual than on any other Monday. Likewise, I advise you consider avoiding terminating someone's employment or laying them off on a Friday to avoid ruining their weekend and allowing them to "stew" for a couple of days. Obviously, any day is a good day to terminate your employee's employment for just cause if they have committed a serious offence. I also recommend that the beginning of a regular work shift is the best time to execute any premeditated employee termination(s) or layoff(s); I suggest doing so at or near the end of a regular work shift is an example of poor taste and *unnecessarily just mean.*

I generally recommend you consider not announcing anyone's employment termination with cause because it may be perceived as boasting and imply your remaining employees should now fear you. An exception to this recommendation may be when your former employee may have committed a serious offence and there is no reasonable chance they may cause any further issue(s) for your business. Believe me, your remaining employees will soon notice and/or discover their fellow ex-employee's absence even without any announcement. I also recommend you openly and honestly reply with the appropriate discretion to anyone's inquiry about the reason(s) for anyone's employment termination while protecting the terminated employee's privacy. I suggest you, as I do, reply with a general response such as "job performance" and let your interested employee(s) come to their own conclusion(s). I also suggest you and your other business leaders may use the period following an ex-employee's termination with cause as an opportunity to reinforce certain company values and/or expectations, as long as you do not appear to be bragging about your ex-employee's departure.

On the other hand, I generally recommend you do announce when an employee(s) has been be laid off or terminated without cause soon after that action(s) has been completed. I suggest you may cause additional unneeded issues for your business and its operations if you make such an announcement before implementing any layoff(s) or termination(s) without cause. I also suggest you, as the business leader, should make this announcement in person or by video to simultaneously communicate to all your employees in several locations. Your personal announcement may reassure your remaining employees that their jobs are secure (for now) and provides you another opportunity to reconfirm current market conditions, the current state of the business, and to tactfully reemphasize what needs to be done by everyone to allow your business to thrive. Perhaps you may find it helpful to explain that it is better to let go a few people versus endangering everyone's jobs. This is a time to be humble, sincere, and compassionate, and to support both your ex-employees who have been laid-off and your remaining employees who will need to "take up the slack."

When terminating any employee with cause, please do not make the mistake (in my opinion) to offer any notice or initially offer financial compensation in lieu of notice. In my opinion, initially offering financial compensation in lieu of notice when terminating an employee with cause may imply the employee is not truly being terminated with cause from a legal viewpoint. As with any employee termination, layoff and employment law situation, I strongly recommend you consult your employment law lawyer before implementing any actions affecting your employees and business.

On the other hand when terminating an employee without cause or permanently laying them off, I generally recommend you do consider offering notice or financial compensation in lieu of notice, unless your business is in extreme financial trouble. You may find offering financial compensation in lieu of notice is more advantageous for your business than just providing notice to your employee. In my opinion, providing only notice may erode the affected employee's morale, which may in turn worsen your remaining employees' morale, who will have a colleague working there as the "walking dead." It is also possible that any employee, depending on their character and/or motives, served with a notice of termination without compensation may be tempted and have an opportunity(ies) to sabotage your business. You never know what people may be capable of, especially when they feel their livelihood is threatened. I recommend you consult your employment law lawyer about how much compensation to offer the affected employee(s) and over what time period.

I suggest you follow the proceedings highlighted in the previous disciplinary procedures section when meeting with your employee(s) affected by a temporary or permanent layoff or a termination with or without cause. I advise you give your affected employee(s) a letter outlining what is happening and why, effective when, what you are offering (if applicable), a time duration to respond to the letter with a legal release (if applicable), and for what time period benefits will be extended (if applicable). I also advise your layoff/termination letter contains your employee's correct address to mail any future employment records, and an offer to provide a good reference (if applicable).

Any employee's resignation, employment termination with or without cause, or temporary/permanent layoff will affect your remaining employees' morale, perhaps in a negative manner in most cases but possibly also in a positive way in other cases. Sometimes your remaining employees may actually thank you, and their morale and thus productivity may dramatically improve after that *rotten apple* employee resigned or whose employment was terminated. From personal experience, I recall one result after a particular supervisor (who no one respected, liked, or got along with) had their employment terminated: an immediate and permanent twenty-percent productivity improvement! In many cases, though, some of your remaining employees' morale may be negatively affected for some time following an ex-employee's resignation, termination, or layoff. I recommend the best way to begin your remaining employees' healing process after their former colleague's departure is to be upfront with them, try to be more available than usual, and speak with any employee(s) who may have any questions and/or concerns. In some situations, you and your other business leaders may need to be *extra* attentive regarding safety, quality, and/or productivity after the departure of an ex-employee(s) as business operations get back to normal, or perhaps improve as soon as possible.

Exit Checklist & Interview

So you have reached the point where an employee(s) is departing from your business; perhaps they have resigned, been terminated with or without cause, or laid off either temporarily or permanently. The loss of employment can be one of the most traumatic events a person can experience in their lives, especially if they were not the event initiator. As I have stated in the previous section, I suggest this is a time when it is critically important to treat your ex-employee(s), or soon-to-be ex-employee(s), and remaining employees, fairly and with compassion. Of course, I also suggest you treat your employees fairly and with respect at all times.

Similar to an onboarding checklist, I recommend you create and implement an exit checklist detailing all the tasks, who is responsible for each task, and the start and end times of each activity to help guide your business through the process of having an employee(s) depart from your company. Your exit checklist should include such items as preparing a plan(s) to redistribute the tasks previously completed by the affected employee(s), consulting your employment law lawyer if necessary, and preparing any letter(s) addressed to the affected employee(s). Your exit checklist should also include items such as getting a good night's sleep the day before and the day of implementing an employee's departure, and announcing the employee's departure to your other business leaders and remaining employees if desired. Finally, your exit checklist should include other items such as retrieving any tools, badges, and other business equipment from the affected employee(s), preparing any documents for your ex-employee(s), conducting an exit interview(s) if feasible, and following up with the affected employee(s) after the event.

Your exit interview, when completed properly and sincerely by both interviewer and exiting employee(s), may serve as an important occasion to follow-up with the affected employee(s) to confirm how they are feeling and adjusting to their new reality. Your exit interview may also be an opportunity to ask your exiting employee(s) how to improve your business in general and its operations. I forewarn you that some exiting or ex-employees may be guarded in their answers, fearing that you may not provide them a good reference(s) in the future. While some ex-employees may provide subtle and/or no clues about how to improve your business, others may have no hesitation to directly tell you why they are leaving and what specific improvements are required in your business.

If feasible and appropriate in a lay-off and/or termination without cause situation, I recommend an appropriate time to conduct an exit interview is when your affected employee(s) returns to your company premises to submit their release form and collect any severance and termination payments. Conducting an exit interview a few days or a week after your ex-employee's departure may be more useful and less stressful than doing so during or soon after their exit when they (and perhaps you as well) may be more emotional and/or upset. I again recommend it is important to be sincere, empathetic, and keep emotions in check during these times. I also advise you never badger and/or negatively criticize an ex-employee in person or after they have left your business. Instead, I advise you to thank your ex-employee(s) for their service, provide constructive criticism if they ask for it, ask if they can be reached for a reasonable period of time in case any remaining employee(s) may have questions for them, offer to follow-up with them to ensure they are okay, and wish them well.

For More Information and Advice

Please contact us at www.chargeupyourpeoplebook.com and/or www.gbicego.com if you would like more information and advice for your human resources challenges such as your employee handbook and policies, disciplinary policies and practices, implementing disciplinary actions, termination and layoff processes, exit checklist and interview and/or any other challenges—we are here to help.

CHAPTER 8

CHANGE

Introduction to Organizational Change

Change is all around us at every moment of our lives. You will find change wherever you look—and if you don't, you may not be looking close enough. The sun's and moon's movements, the seasons, the weather, everything in nature, and even in our physical bodies, are in a constant state of change. I suggest your perspective of change depends only on your point of view; this explains why some people may notice, not notice, like, or dislike any change(s). From my experiences (and perhaps your own as well), many people may not like, or prefer, some change(s), at least when it/they first occur —it may seem unfamiliar, strange, and downright scary at times. I suggest we may all view any change(s) as good/bad or as favourable/ unfavourable, depending on our point of view and goals. I also suggest each person's degree of accepting or rejecting any change(s) is determined by their own values and beliefs. This is why leading organizational change(s) may be particularly challenging for any business leader.

Change(s) may be categorized as mandatory or voluntary. Some organizational changes are mandatory and relatively easy to implement because there is nothing anyone can practically do about them. For example, some law(s) may be enacted in your business jurisdiction starting on a specific date that requires a certain policy or practice affecting everyone in your company and/or your business's operations. The vast majority, if not all, businesses and their employees comply with the new law(s) unless they prefer risking to suffer the consequences of not doing so. On the contrast, implementing voluntary organizational changes can be much more challenging; this is when you, as a business leader, must rely on and use other means to ensure compliance from your employees. The remainder of this chapter will focus on how to effectively implement positive, voluntary, and long-lasting organizational change.

I recommend there are at least three requirements to implement positive, effective, and long-lasting organizational change(s): avoid the temptation to change just for the sake of change, identify a reason(s) for change, and consider the WIIFM (What's In It For Me) factor. Let's discuss each of these requirements below.

Requirements for Effective Organizational Change

The first of at least three requirements to implement positive, effective, and long-lasting organizational change(s) is to avoid the temptation to change or adjust anything and/or everything just for the sake of change. I suggest you may consider at times not doing anything to alter a long-standing policy, practice, or method that seems to work well. A well-established policy or practice may have already passed the test of time, been tweaked, changed, modified, and optimized to a point where any further investment of time, efforts, capital, and other resources may result in diminishing returns. If this is the case, I recommend you leave that time-tested policy, practice, or method unchanged for now and focus your continuous improvement efforts and activities on other higher-priority challenges.

The second of at least three requirements for positive, effective, and long-lasting organizational change(s) is to identify a reason(s) or motivation(s) for its implementation. Motivation may be classified as positive or negative, or in others terms as "the carrot or the stick." Positive or *carrot* motivation is the desire to improve your present and/or future circumstance(s), whereas negative or stick motivation is the desire to avoid some unpleasant potential condition(s) in the present and/or future. You need to determine which type of motivation is more powerful to encourage your organization to follow and implement change. I recommend you consider using a combination of both positive and negative motivations to lead positive, effective, and enduring organizational change(s) within your business.

The last of at least three requirements for positive, effective, long lasting organizational change is to always consider the WIIFM (What's In It For Me) factor for each individual and/or group of employees and other people directly and indirectly affected by the change(s). It is obvious that the probability of implementing any voluntary and long-term change(s) affecting others improves as others recognize new or enhanced benefits for themselves and/or no erosion or elimination of current benefits as a result(s) of the change(s). As much as you would like to think that a change initiator may act only for the benefit of others, some people may initiate change(s) that may benefit others and also themselves—in some cases, unfortunately, only themselves.

Implementing Organizational Change

The process of leading and accepting a voluntary organizational change(s) typically occurs through at least three stages: resistance, consideration, and acceptance. At first, some employees may literally try to ignore an organizational change. Some people may try to defend their resistance due to their own viewpoint(s), justification(s), and belief(s), and may even try to ridicule your new initiative(s) with comments such as, "It will never work," or "This is crazy." It is critical at this point that you continue implementing your change(s) with tenacity, and I suggest your leadership credibility and ability to implement any future change(s) may suffer if you abandon your change efforts at the first sign(s) of resistance. Your persistence may be rewarded when your employees reach the second stage of change when they begin considering your new change(s) may actually *work* and/or may be beneficial to them and/or the business. I recommend you continue to focus, at every stage of implementing change, on emphasizing the benefits for everyone involved or affected by the change(s). As usual, most people are typically interested in the WIIFM (What's In It For Me) factor, so I advise you focus on the benefits that address peoples' concerns. Since different people may have different viewpoints, goals, values and beliefs, I advise you emphasize a combination or variety of benefits to each audience accordingly. The final stage of implementing voluntary organizational change(s) is acceptance of that change(s). At this point, I recommend you continue emphasizing the benefits of such change(s) but not as aggressively as during the previous two stages, or you may risk "tiring out" or exhausting some employees. Once you confirm your new change(s) has taken effect, it's time to focus on other priorities as you continue monitoring your employees' compliance to your recent new change(s).

Most people also react to a new change(s) depending on their personality type which can be categorized in four groups: the *casualty*, the *spectator*, the *criticizer*, or the *supporter*. The *casualty* is a person who may initially think that every change(s) is aimed at them and their own detriment, and that they are a victims of others' actions and decisions. The *casualty* may eventually comply with any new change(s) while continuing to view it/them as something(s) they have no control over, including their own reaction(s) to such change(s). The *spectator* is a person who may seem neutral, neither opposed or supportive, of any change(s)—they may just watch from the sidelines as everyone else complies with the new change(s). The *spectator* may also comply with any new change(s) sooner than the *casualty* and the *criticizer*. The *criticizer* is obviously a person who directly and/or indirectly opposes any new change(s) using their verbal and nonverbal means of communications. Many of your employees may be a *casualty*, *spectator*, or *criticizer*. You may need to use more negative motivation for the *casualty* and the *criticizer*, a balance of both negative and positive motivations for the *spectator*, and more positive motivation for the *supporter* to accept new change(s). The *supporter* is a person(s) who is encouraged by and readily accepts your new change(s), and may also be an active advocate(s) of the new policy(ies) or practice(s). You may also find that your *supporters* may be asking for more and quicker change(s) depending on their point(s) of view(s).

Your change *supporters* play a critical role(s) to help you and your business leaders implement change(s) throughout your company. In fact, your first *supporter's* or *follower's* support may be more critical than the change initiator's backing because the change leader usually already believes in the new change(s). I suggest true acceptance of any new change(s) actually begins when your other employees witness the genuine support by another *supporter* employee(s) who may have just as much (or perhaps more in some ways) credibility than you do with them. I recommend you first and quickly focus your efforts to convince your potential *supporter* employees of a new change(s) to accelerate acceptance throughout your entire business. I also suggest you may have different *supporter* employees for different changes depending on their values, beliefs, goals, and viewpoints.

As the overall business leader, I recommend you always monitor the accumulative rate of change and the effects of each and all change(s) within your organization regardless if change(s) sources(s) are internal and/or external to your business. There may be a limit(s) of how much and how quickly your business, employees, customers, and suppliers may absorb change(s). I advise that trying to implement what eventually turns out to be too little or too much change may frustrate both change initiators and those affected by change(s). Implementing too much change may create an obstacle(s) for further change(s) that may be more critical or important to the success of your business. And implementing too little change may jeopardize your chances to achieve your business goals and objectives.

I also recommend you constantly monitor your employees' morale and ask for their feedback to assess if your current rate of accumulative change is meeting your business's needs. I also suggest you adjust your business accumulative rate of change to a point that it is challenging, and perhaps slightly out of reach, to encourage your business to "stretch" without becoming totally and permanently overwhelming, thus "bogging down" your business operations. At first, a change(s) may introduce a shock to your business which may not be a bad thing, as long as this *shock(s)* is temporary and entices your employees to exercise a new behaviour(s). I suggest it may be prudent to consider allowing your business and employees *catch their breath* before implementing your next change(s), depending on your own business objectives. I also recommend you do not allow too much time to pass between successive changes that may result in a reduced momentum to implement further improvements and/or tempt your employees to become comfortable with your new business status quo.

You as a Change Agent

A change agent is recognized by others as leading an initiative(s) that will alter an organization, for better or for worse. You, as the general business leader, may typically be expected and decide to be your company's overall change agent due to your overall vision for and authority in your organization. You may have other change agents within and outside of your business, both in formal and informal capacities that can be or become more effective change agents than yourself for some issues. In these cases, I suggest you consider focusing your initial efforts to influence your other business change agents to effect change(s) throughout your entire organization. There are at least eight characteristics common to every successful change agent similar to those required for effective leadership.

One required change agent characteristic is vision—you must first have or start with a clear idea and foresight within your own mind about the intended change(s), the reasons(s), motivation(s), and benefit(s) of the change(s) for your business. I suggest you think about this: how can you or anyone convince or entice others to comply with or follow any change(s) if you are not clear about it/them yourself? I recommend you simplify your vision as much as possible to maximize its effectiveness and chances to be accepted, implemented, and endure over the long term.

A second common change agent trait is the ability to effectively communicate how and when your new vision and change(s) will benefit your business and everyone affected by it/them. This is when you need to rely on both your verbal and nonverbal communication skills to correspond with your employees, customers, and suppliers how the change(s) will benefit the business and them. You may also find it necessary to use your conflict management skills to resolve any competing priorities between your employees, customers, and suppliers when implementing a change(s). I recommend you always decide on a course of action(s) that eventually benefits your business.

A third change agent common characteristic is consistency, i.e. consistent adherence to your vision and goals. Your consistency in your efforts to implementing organizational change(s) is based upon your faith, belief, and hope that the benefits to your business will be more important than any issue(s) that may arise due to the change(s). Being consistent when implementing change can be thought of as waves hitting a shoreline, constantly back and forth. As a change agent, it may first seem as a constant battle or struggle that you must consistently communicate your vision and goals (waves) with your organization (shoreline). I suggest you consider that your consistent adherence to your vision and goals will eventually shape your business, just as waves hitting a shoreline eventually form that shoreline.

A fourth characteristic of all successful change agents is remaining flexible on how to achieve your vision and/or goals. While remaining consistent in your vision and goals, the degree of your flexibility to consider and implement other peoples' ideas and methods to achieve your vision or goals will determine how quickly and effectively new change(s) may be implemented and adhered to by your employees over the long term.

A fifth common characteristic of every successful change agent is their ability to effectively involve employees in every change(s). Without genuine employee involvement, you may revert to implementing a *mandatory* change(s) with its/their associated increased resistance and enforcement requirements. Authentic employee involvement just makes so much sense, especially when you, as a change agent, want to implement voluntary organizational change(s) that will pass the test of time without your personal continued involvement and/or enforcement.

A sixth successful change agent common characteristic is the courage to think and act that may at times challenge the current status quo. I recommend you demonstrate respect for certain status quo issues while challenging them at the same time. Your courage as a change agent may be demonstrated by your ability to ask *tough* questions and propose what may initially seem like challenging solutions.

A seventh change agent common characteristic is the need to be a knowledgeable problem solver. As an effective change agent, you must have and demonstrate sufficient experience and knowledge to implement solutions to the various challenges that may be anticipated and/or will reveal themselves when implementing change(s). I also recommend you do not hesitate to initially say, "I'm not sure," or "I don't know," when you are genuinely tested by a specific question or challenge. In this case, I advise you then seek out and follow-up with an appropriate answer(s) and/or solution(s). Most people will appreciate your honesty and integrity when conducting your affairs in such a manner.

An eighth common characteristic of every successful and effective change agent is honesty and its related characteristic of integrity. I propose there are no "shades" of a person's honesty and integrity, i.e.

it is not possible and/or acceptable that a person may be "a little" honest or dishonest. Similar to the quote, *"How you do anything is how you do everything,"* I suggest a person is either honest or not honest— there is no "in between." But how can you address a question asked by an employee that requires you to disclose some perhaps confidential information that may not be appropriate and/or you are not permitted to divulge? In this case, I recommend you remain honest and consider replying that it would not be appropriate and/or you are not permitted to disclose information that would be part of your honest answer. I recommend you always maintain your honesty and integrity since they are two of your most important characteristics of being recognized as a successful and effective change leader.

For More Information and Advice

Please contact us at www.chargeupyourpeoplebook.com and/or www.gbicego.com if you would like more information and advice for your change challenges such as organizational change, requirements for and implementing effective organizational change, being a successful change agent and/or any other challenges—we are here to help.

CHAPTER 9

THE END & YOUR NEW BEGINNING

It May Not Be So Bad

The end of a business, job, or any stage in life may not be the "end of your life." I suggest the only real "end of your life" will occur when you physically die, and that only happens once! So, why do many people seem to interpret the end of a business or a job as such a *serious* or *bad* life-changing event? I suggest there's only one reason: fear. Fear of not being able to financially support themselves, their family, friends, charitable causes and lifestyle, fear of not knowing what to do with themselves, uncertainty, loneliness, fear of losing or reducing their social status or being judged, fear of failure and/or success. The list of potential and real human fears may seem endless. You may have, at times, personally felt these fears and know many other people who have as well—this is normal and part of our human condition in my opinion.

I suggest you consider the viewpoint that all changes, especially external ones occurring outside of your personal control, are neutral, i.e. they can be interpreted as *good* or *bad*, or perhaps even *good* and *bad*. I also suggest your interpretation of all changes, especially external ones, depends on your viewpoints, beliefs, values, and goals in your particular arena(s) of life that may be affected by the change(s). For example, a marketplace change could threaten your current product and/or service but may also provide an opportunity for your business to quickly react and take advantage of it to further grow your revenues. In another example, the resignation of a senior leader in your organization my affect your business in the short term but can also pave the way to chart a new direction(s) leading to expanded business growth.

I also advise you reflect upon the philosophy that you either grow or "die" both in business and in life— not physically die, but "die" in a manner(s) that you cease to grow, and become one of the "walking dead." You know, one of those people who get up every morning, get ready to go to their business/job, go to work, then work, work, work, work, come home, spend some time (if any) with family or friends, perhaps watch some TV, and go to bed. Then they repeat their routine the next day, and the next, and the next day after that, until they reach the weekend and perhaps fall into some other routine(s) repeated on a regular basis. Some people describe this kind of life as *living in quiet desperation*. There may be a time in any business activity, whether you're leading or working in a company, when you may conclude it is best that you stop that activity for your own and/or the business's benefit. At first, such a change may seem scary, or down-right frightening, and *unthinkable*, but may be absolutely invaluable for your long term success and happiness as the end of one phase/activity can be the beginning of a whole new and better life and/or world.

Job End Early Warning Signs

If you are employed by someone else in their business, there may be early warning signs you are no longer growing within that company and perhaps "on your way out." You can decide to either pay attention to or just ignore these early warning signs that your employment will end sooner or later. It may not seem fair at first, and/or frustrating while you try to understand what "you have done wrong" and/or what may have happened to make you feel and think your employment will soon end. I recommend you always be on the lookout for any of these signs and then act accordingly. Employment end early warning signs can be classified as internal (caused by you) or external (caused by others).

Internal employment end early warning signs may be more obvious as you begin to think and feel you may want or need to quit your job. An obvious sign is when you find it difficult to wake up and be motivated to go to work over a long period of time. I'm not necessarily talking about the occasional Sunday night "so sad tomorrow is Monday" syndrome, although this too can be significant enough for you to consider finding another place to work. I suggest we all experience days or times when we *just don't feel like going to work*, regardless if you work for someone else or lead your own business. It may be time for you to start thinking about either remaining in your current job to fix any issue(s), or just leave, if you find it increasingly mentally difficult to even get to work over a sustained period of time. A related and more obvious and alarming warning sign is that you may just not care anymore about your job and your employer's business. "I don't care" thinking can be more dangerous than the "Sunday night sadness" syndrome since it may cause substandard performance that may be quickly noticed by others.

Other internal employment end early warning signs may include boredom in your current job and/or you may not have grown both professionally and personally in your current job over a long period of time. Even worse, you may conclude you are "burnt out"—in this case, I recommend you immediately reach out to family, friends, mental and/or physical health professionals, or anyone else to help you heal yourself before experiencing any further potential health issues. And finally, it may occur that you sense your *gut feeling* is telling you it's time to go—sometimes you just "know that you know" that it may be time to start looking for other employment.

External employment end early warning signs may be more subtle than your internal ones. Sometimes one of these external employment end warning signs may not be cause for concern and/or a misinterpretation on your part, but I recommend you consider starting to update your resume if you begin noticing several of these signs over time. Examples of external employment end early warning signs may include not obtaining a promotion, poor or sometimes unusually harsh performance reviews, comments, or criticism from your supervisor and/or others, suddenly not being invited to participate in business retreats that you usually attended in the past, going on business trips or having others attending in your place, and the loss of other perks. Additional examples may include you not receiving any pay or benefits increases or bonuses whereas they are given to others, being asked to take some time off, more than usual detailed reviews of how you spend your time and your expense reports, and being assigned fewer and less high profile projects. A new senior leadership and/or change of business ownership may also raise the possibility of the new management hiring their own people they've worked with in the past or, even worse, personal friends, to replace you and others in your current positions.

Further examples of external employment end early warning signs include loss of support staff, fewer responsibilities, being micromanaged or ignored all together, strange behaviour(s) from your co-workers, gradually being excluded from discussions, emails, meetings, and decisions that you used to be a part of, or your access to data has been restricted. More disturbing and perhaps aggravating signs your job may be in jeopardy is when your supervisor and/or others bypass you and go directly to your team members for various issues, or (worse in my opinion) when a person is transferred into your business who may or may not officially or unofficially report to you as a business leader. Some of these actions may be explained at first as sincere ways to help you and/or improve the company; regardless, I recommend you monitor your situation very carefully and consider your options going forward.

Business End Early Warning Signs

Some early business end early warning signs can be considered similar to those for employment end early warning signs, except that you can substitute a supervisor for a job in the above examples with a banker, customer, and/or any significant business stakeholder. Business end early warning signs can be classified as financial or non-financial.

Potential financial business end warning signs are relatively more obvious than non-financial ones. The most obvious and classic financial business end early warning sign is cash flow challenges, e.g. when it is difficult to pay bills on time, accounts receivables are out of control, or a business may run out of money for further expansion. Other examples include significant gross and/or net margin reduction(s), sales losses, an increase of bad debts, market share losses due to new technology, competitors, and/or an unanticipated market shift(s). Additional financial business end early warning sign examples consist of a loss of customers and/or less interaction and communication with customers such as not being invited to bid new projects.

Non-financial business end warning signs may be more subtle in nature and more imperative to monitor since successfully dealing with these ones will improve your chances of avoiding the more serious financial ones. Examples include consistent low employee morale, excessive employee absenteeism, and high employee turnover, especially from *star* employees, an increase in the frequency and severity of accidents, increased quality problems both internally within the business and reaching customers, and an increase in late deliveries. Other non-financial business end warning signs may include excessive increases in production costs such as overtime, scrap, and equipment downtime, reduction of people and money investments into marketing and sales, and research and development initiatives. Additional examples may consist of prolonged animosity amongst business partners or members of the board of directors, a lack of business leadership focus, and not seeking or using professional advice.

Ending Your Business or Employment

Ending your business either by transferring/selling it to someone else/another business or declaring bankruptcy, or ending your employment either by your own or your employers' decision can be a very sad life event. But I also suggest this event may be very invigorating and revitalizing in some cases. I recommend you consider all options and solutions to your situation before you voluntarily decide to end your business or employment in someone else's business. If and when you do decide to end your business or employment, I have the following pieces of advice.

Always act professionally right to the end, i.e. keep running your business and do your job, and more, until the very last minute. Although circumstances may seem to justify any bitterness, resentfulness, and/or frustration(s), I recommend you always treat others with respect, especially during these challenging times. If you are ending your business, I also suggest you provide your employees, customers, and suppliers with as much warning as possible so they can make other arrangements for themselves. Similarly, I advise you provide your current employer as much lead-time for your departure as possible to give them ample time to find your replacement and/or reorganize as they see fit. In these and many other situations, I suggest people will appreciate your candor and being forthright with them.

I also recommend you have sufficient financial resources to sustain yourself, family, and other significant financial obligations before ending your business or resigning from your job. It may be ideal, depending on your short term goals and objectives, that you have obtained another business and/or job before leaving your current one. I also suggest you speak with and obtain advice from your closest family, friends, and other trusted advisors before deciding to end your business or resign from your job. And once you've decided and actually closed your business or resigned from your job, I recommend you do not "burn any bridges," learn from your experience(s), and move on to your life's next adventure(s).

Your New Beginning

The beginning of any new event can be a very exciting time in life, such as the birth of a child, a new season, experience, job, or starting a new business. It can be a time filled with the excitement of the unknown, doing something different, broadening your horizons, and growing as a person. At the same time, you may also feel worry, panic, and/or apprehension that your decision and subsequent action(s) may involve some or too much risk. I recommend you, as I do, treasure these times in life. Below are a few tips or advice to consider when you find yourself at a new life beginning.

I suggest it is okay if you initially feel sad, angry, and/or depressed, especially if your new life beginning is not a result of your own decision(s). I also recommend you may find it beneficial to speak to family, friends, trusted advisors, health professionals, or anyone else if you feel any emotions of anxiety and/or depression that are intense and/or last for some time. You be the judge for yourself and decide what makes sense to you—everyone is different.

I also recommend you be careful not to regress and to be by yourself for long and/or excessive periods of time. Owning and/or running a business or having a job is typically a very social activity. How many people do you know who meet with their business and/or work ex-colleagues many years after some or all of them have disbanded from a particular company? I suggest they may do so because they have developed personal relationships that have gone beyond work or the business. To combat loneliness, I advise you reach out to your partner, your family, and friends, or volunteer your time at a local charitable organization, or just go for a walk to stay in contact with other people.

I also advise you continue your daily routine activities not associated with leading a business or working in a job. Such activities may include contact with family and friends, daily exercise, or grabbing a coffee or tea at a local restaurant(s). I suggest continuing your daily activities, outside of business or work, plays an important part to "keep you grounded" and provides a sense of continuance of your daily life, i.e. that your world is not "coming to an end."

At the same time, I recommend you consider taking some "time off" to rest and enjoy yourself as much as you need or can afford to; everyone is different so I suggest only you know how much rest and time off satisfies your needs. The transition time between businesses and/or jobs is an excellent opportunity to reflect upon your life priorities and progress. This is an excellent occasion to take some time for yourself and reflect on what you want to do with your time, your life, and what really does and does not matter to you. You may also want to read a book(s), write a journal, go for a long walk, take a vacation, or pursue whatever physical activity helps relax you and gets your mind off whatever event(s) has/have happened in your life.

I urge you to start designing your life as soon as you shed any issues associated with your past business and/or job! Dare to be open minded—think "out of the box!" Think about what you've always wanted to do, what really *turns you on* and then start to write down and work on your goals. As each day passes, your new goals may begin to take shape and become part of your new daily reality, and you will find yourself on your way to a new business, a new job, and a new life!

Congratulations, enjoy the ride, and help others to do the same!

For More Information and Advice

Please contact us at www.chargeupyourpeoplebook.com and/or www.gbicego.com if you would like more information and advice for your business or employment early warning signs, ending your business or employment, your new beginning and/or any other challenges—we are here to help.

ABOUT THE AUTHOR

Giorgio Bicego has spent 30+ years helping his clients and employers achieve and exceed their business objectives within roles such as Vice President Operations, General Manager, Lean Facilitator, Business Manager, Senior Program Manager, Plant Manager, Assistant Quality Manager, Process Engineering Manager, and Health & Safety and Environment Manager. Giorgio has directed and guided businesses, designed, led and implemented projects and initiatives resulting in both new annual sales and annual cost savings ranging up to tens and hundreds of thousands, and tens and hundreds of millions, of dollars in Canada, the USA, Mexico, parts of Europe, and East Asia.

In addition to authoring several books and other programs, Giorgio also shares his strategies and ideas as a consultant, coach, mentor, instructor, trainer, and speaker.

Giorgio has been described as an energetic, driven, bottom-line, results-oriented, flexible, pragmatic, *hands-on* problem solver and change agent who is systems-orientated while continuously seeking to eliminate waste. While being a long-term planner, Giorgio is also able to think quickly on his feet, is proactive and able to identify issues and their resolutions using his excellent leadership, communications, negotiation, organizational, analytical, and commercial skills. Throughout his career, Giorgio has been liked and well respected by his clients, employees, employers, customers, suppliers, shareholders, and students.

Giorgio has contributed to, and improved, his clients' and employers' businesses in the areas of leadership, commercial management, profit and loss performance, turn-arounds, strategic planning, financial analyses, budgets, organization/systems development, and project management. Giorgio has also designed and led business development, marketing, account management, customer service, supply chain, distribution, and new and innovative product design and development initiatives. Giorgio has extensive experience in, and has led, operations, materials management (order and release management, scheduling, capacity and resource planning, inventory control, procurement, logistics), finance, cost control, quality, production, delivery, engineering, maintenance, facilities, health and safety, environment, human resources, and customer liaison projects. Finally, Giorgio has successfully directed many programs in lean manufacturing, world class manufacturing (WCM), Kaizen, 5S, TPM, VSM, OEE, SMED, cellular manufacturing, one-piece flow, visual management, Kaizen Teian, metrics, ISO 9001/2 & 14001, TS16949, and is familiar with HACCP, GMP concepts and system requirements.

Giorgio has also been described as a focused, confident, and transparent leader who is passionate about improving employee morale, fostering employee empowerment, and creating harmonious business environments under sometimes very challenging circumstances. His unique understanding of human nature, insights, experiences, and extensive people skills have permitted him to dramatically improve an individual's, and groups of individual's, attitudes and motivations to fully contribute to business's successes. With his authentic, open-minded, and innovative approaches, Giorgio has been able to work with all types of people, take charge of challenging situations, and propel businesses and their employees into new and long lasting periods of continuous improvements. Along the way, Giorgio also inspires, teaches, and coaches others to reach their human potential, not only as leaders and employees but as people outside of their work environments.

Contact Giorgio at www.chargeupyourpeoplebook.com and/or www.gbicego.com for:

- more information, advice, and help with your business and people challenges
- coaching and mentoring needs
- training and instruction requirements
- speaking engagements

ADDITIONAL RESOURCES

www.chargeupyourbusinessbook.com
www.chargeupyourpeoplebook.com

B A

BICEGO & ASSOCIATES

Linked in

www.gbicego.com
www.linkedin.com/in/giorgio-bicego-61386111/